Build Your Own Life

about the author

Wendy Lawson Bss. Bsw (Hons) Gdip (psychstud) Gdip (pyschology) is currently working for her PhD in Health Science at Deakin University, Warrnambool in Australia. Her topic is 'Autism and Stress'. Wendy is no stranger to stress and anxiety both of which haunt her life on a daily basis. However, Wendy, a mother of four, who was originally diagnosed as being intellectually disabled, then in her teens, as being schizophrenic, and finally in 1994, as having an autism spectrum disorder, is learning to take control of her life and is finding ways to share her knowledge and experience with others. 'Build Your Own Life' is an echo that should be heard on every street corner and in every back yard. In understanding how to build our own lives and relate to the community around us, we are building a better, safer world where autonomy and confidence can reign. Wendy is an author of four books, including 'Life Behind Glass' (her autobiography) and Understanding and Working with the Spectrum of Autism. Her youngest son, now 21 years of age, was diagnosed at the age of 12, as having Asperger's Syndrome. Tim loves Rotary engines and proudly drives his 1978 RX7. Wendy prefers piston engines. It takes both kinds of engine to drive a world of difference!

also by Wendy Lawson

**Understanding and Working with the Spectrum
of Autism
An Insider's View**
ISBN 1 85302 971 8

**Life Behind Glass
A Personal Account of Autism Spectrum Disorder**
ISBN 1 85302 911 4

Build Your Own Life:
A Self-Help Guide For
Individuals With Asperger's
Syndrome

Wendy Lawson

Illustrations by Elizabeth Walker

Jessica Kingsley Publishers
London and Philadelphia

First published in the United Kingdom in 2003
by Jessica Kingsley Publishers
116 Pentonville Road
London N1 9JB, England
and
400 Market Street, Suite 400
Philadelphia, PA 19106, USA

www.jkp.com

Copyright © Wendy Lawson 2003
Second impression 2003
Third impression 2004

Library of Congress Cataloging in Publication Data
A CIP catalog record for this book is available from the Library of Congress

British Library Cataloguing in Publication Data
A CIP catalogue record for this book is available from the British Library

ISBN 1 84310 114 9

Printed and Bound in Great Britain by
Athenaeum Press, Gateshead, Tyne and Wear

Contents

Foreword

Having known and worked with Wendy for some years now, I am delighted to write the foreword to this, her fourth book.

Wendy worked extremely hard for years to piece together her fragmented experiences of the world. The things people told her usually made no sense. So she had to understand life for herself, 'from the ground up'. Because things which seemed obvious to other people did not seem obvious to her, Wendy has been a 'clear-eyed' and scrupulous observer. She has noticed that many of her own difficulties have undermined her confidence, and have been made worse by negativity from other people. Rather than giving in to that she has developed resources to deal with it.

Since Wendy was identified as being on the Autism Spectrum, she has realised that many of the problems she experiences are widespread. That realisation has inspired a personal quest to pass her own hard–won understanding on to everybody else concerned, in the hope that much suffering may be avoided. Wendy and I first met at a 'Positive Autism' conference in East London where we were both presenting (I with my colleague Mike Lesser). Our message to the conference was essentially the same, namely that being 'single-channelled' (Wendy's term) or 'monotropic' (my term) rather than multi-channelled or polytropic was the key difference between autistic and typical people. Since then Wendy and I have toured, presented, and debated together as often as geographical distance permits, and are hoping to publish with Lesser some thoughts on monotropism and the diagnostic criteria.

Wendy's previous books have been devoted to explaining autism to the non-autistic and offering constructive ideas to improve relations between them. In this book her constructive outlook is offered directly to other people on the Autism spectrum. With the use of an extended metaphor, Wendy shares her understanding of how to take control of your own life and strengthen it against life's storms. Thus strengthened, anyone may feel brave enough to venture out like Wendy and prove their value in the world outside.

Dinah Murray

Dr. Dinah Murray is a Person Centred Consultant to adults with an Autism Spectrum Disorder, a supportive friend to Wendy and to many others. Dinah has published many papers on Autism, and written course units for Birmingham University's Distance Education and Web based courses in Autism, for which she is a tutor.

Wendy, Asperger's Syndrome
and neurotypicality

Asperger's Syndrome (AS) is not a disease, but a developmental disorder (difference) that enables individuals to process life quite differently from that of typical individuals. Asperger's Syndrome is an autism spectrum disorder, or difference (ASD).

As a child and teenager I lived with much confusion, anxiety, fear and distress, mostly because I found the world around me too difficult to figure out and relate to. As an adult I took refuge in living a more sheltered life, in the country and away from too much demand. I went to church, raised my children and spent long hours writing, listening and studying other people. I was eventually diagnosed with Asperger's Syndrome in August 1994 when I was 42 years of age.

When we look at the various diagnostic criteria for Asperger's Syndrome we see a common thread. Each one picks up on our difficulties with social interaction, communication and tendency towards specific interests. The Diagnostic and Statistical Manual of Mental Disorders, 4th edition (DSM-1V), (American Psychiatric Association 1994), states that Asperger's Syndrome (referred to there as Asperger's Disorder) is diagnosed when all the typical signs of Autism are present, but the individual has normal language development. In order to qualify for a diagnosis of Autism/Asperger an individual needs to show a divergence away from the typical, spanning three broad areas: social interaction, communication and rigid thinking. The cluster must contain at least two signs indicating social interaction difficulties, and one indication in each of the communication and stereotyped patterns of behaviour categories. Also the pattern unfolding must clearly be not typical of other disorders, such as schizophrenia or one of the other pervasive developmental disorders. In practical terms this might mean we dislike change (we prefer routine); we tend to be obsessive; we become anxious very easily and we may take what is said to us literally (for example: wife says to John, her husband "Can you invite Jim over for dinner?" "Yes" says John. However, John fails to give Jim the invitation. When questioned about this John replies "You didn't ask me to actually invite Jim, you just asked me if I could").

However, along with some of my colleagues (Dinah Murray, Mike Lesser, Donna Williams and Temple Grandin) I believe that individuals with AS are single minded (or have one tracked minds) and that we process information in bits, piece by piece or one at a time. Murray calls this 'monotropism' and I reckon this explains my difficulties and my strengths very well. If we look at the DSM-IV criteria, monotropism can account for all the areas mentioned. This could mean that we have an eye for the detail that typical individuals may miss, but sometimes we may fail to connect to the bigger picture.

The term 'neurotypical' can be applied to individuals preoccupied with social demands, appearances, public image, wearing of the 'right' clothes and conversing only about things that appear to be 'in their interest'. OK this might seem a bit harsh, but this is how many typical/neurotypical individuals appear to be. If you do not meet the criteria for ASD the chances are that you will be a typical person, sometimes referred to as neurotypical (NT). In this book neurotypical and typical are used interchangeably. To see if you fit the criteria for a diagnosis of neurotypicality visit the following web site: http://isnt.autistics.org/cgi-exec/test/test.cgi

As an NT person you will have the capacity to multi-channel information and process many different things almost at once. For example during a conversation you will probably be able to look at someone and listen to them simultaneously. Murray calls this 'polytropism'. I believe that these differences in how we each encounter life are the core issues that separate us. Once, however, we understand these things about each other and we can work together to accommodate them we will all be less stressed people!

Some useful internet sites

> www.autismandcomputing.org.uk
>
> www.mugsy.org/wendy
>
> www.users.dircon.co.uk/~cns/
>
> www.asperger-syndrome.com

Acknowledgements

Before I could venture out and explore the building of my own life, I needed to experience a sense of my own 'being' and of that 'being' as someone who is of value. To love and accept oneself one must know love and acceptance of others. This knowledge and understanding is under constant threat as the inevitable 'failures', mistakes and inappropriate decisions of daily life become tangled in the cement of my foundations. However, I am learning that even an insecurity or a fear can be encountered as a positive venture when welcomed as a challenge and not a foe. I owe my continuing discovery of 'self' and my humanness to those friends and family who have supported me over the years. None of us is an island. The life I choose to build is one of interdependence and I am thankful to every other human being who is a current part of who I am today. You know who you are. Thank you.

Special appreciation goes to Judy Mason whose support during our metaphor writing episodes for this book meant hours of hilarity and shared tears! So many have contributed to this book with their comments, interest and time, thank you. Just knowing you are out there and that you care, is a lifetime's treasure.

Introduction

Build your own life is all about the realisation that we are all different. However, individuals with Asperger's Syndrome can be so different from the average group that our language, interests, and culture appear to be alien to many people. As one of these aliens I would suggest that we experience life in a way that enables us to focus, but in a way that many others do not fully understand. This book is written in an attempt to help my fellow aliens familiarise ourselves, as aliens, with a better understanding of ourselves and of others. If you like, it is an attempt to work out and make sense of our lives, and the lives of so many around us.

I am writing as one individual to another to share from my experiences in the hope that we can build a shared mutual identity, as well as some common understanding. When I woke up from sleep this morning I remembered a dream that I had during the night. In the dream I saw a group of people at a friend's house. I was amongst the group moving between the people as they talked to one another. I realised that although I thought of these individuals as 'my friends' we really had little 'in common' with one another. I was (am) autistic, they were (are) neurotypical or non-autistic. They could talk together with ease about many different topics. I talk easily, but only about topics that interest me. In fact, although we talk together with ease when I am with any one of these 'friends' on our own, in the group they talk more with one another than with me. I am a friend as an individual on many occasions, but I am not chosen as a person to be with when there are others who can share more of the 'common' interest than I can. I am mentioning this not as a complaint but as a fact. It is the reasoning for this behaviour and many other aspects of what it means to be a person on the autism spectrum that I hope this book will help to clarify.

Whilst growing up I experienced many occasions when individuals said and did things that I didn't understand. 'Wendy, answer the question,' Teacher might say. 'Oh, I cannot answer the question Miss, but Christine can. She answers more questions in class than anyone else,' I replied. This to me seemed a reasonable and logical answer. Yet, for being honest I was sent to the head teacher for being rude. I thought being rude was when you didn't say please or thank you. Or, sometimes I was told that I was to stop being rude when I looked at the paper over someone's shoulder on the bus. I couldn't understand how it was rude to be honest! This is the kind of neurotypical reasoning we will explore in this book.

To understand the 'what', 'why' and 'wherefore' of many of the individuals we meet and those we share our lives with, we need to understand their diagnosis or their neurotypicality. We will use the terms associated with mapping, such as roads, roundabouts, junctions and so on, to enable exploration of life directions and possibilities. We will use the term 'building' or 'house', when we refer to ourselves. I hope that as we travel through the contents of this book together the actions and words of people around us will make more sense. In exploring their words, terminology and events we might discover the various crossroads that metaphors direct us to and interpret them. We will visit the junctions of decision making and problem solving and uncover their potential. We will locate the 'roundabouts' of possible life directions and map them out. This book is intended to be a map, a tool to look things up and interpret them, a guide in our mutual life journey. We will be exploring words, not on their own, but rather their connections to us, others and to life.

We won't find every answer in this book to every problem that we encounter. However, we will be able to decipher many of the verbal encounters we experience and at least understand their content and their implications. Even the non-verbal communication that neurotypical individuals use constantly (their facial expressions and the bodily movements that often accompany their words but sometimes occur without words) will be explored in the following chapters.

In Chapter 1 (Foundations for life) we will look at what the foundations are that separate us from the typical people. In many ways you and I are actually designed quite differently to neurotypical individuals. We are put together differently in the way that we process life encounters and in the way we move from processing to understanding and to eventual outcomes. It is important to understand their difference because it will explain much of what they do, why they do it and why they expect us to do it too. If we get our foundations right, our building will stand firm and will weather most storms. The building can, if you like, be a symbol for 'you' and for 'me'. When I write about 'the building', I am describing metaphorically the building of who we are. We are each like a building. Some individuals may think of themselves as a house standing tall and firm in a street quite alone from all the other houses. Others will imagine hobbit homes. The important factor is that your house is a safe place to venture out from and back into.

Which 'home' do you think represents you?

Whenever a house is being constructed the foundations are laid first. After our foundations are finished we use them to start the process of building the walls of who we are. Chapter 2 (Designing, planning and structuring our building) demonstrates this procedure as it explores the various types of scaffolding constructed upon the foundations to secure the framework for the rest of the building. We all need support in life. It is OK to need other people in our lives. This chapter explores what our needs might be, what the needs of others might be, how we can negotiate having those needs met and how we can protect ourselves during the process.

Every building has spaces within it. These spaces might be called rooms. Rooms are built for various purposes. Chapter 3 (Erecting the building) explores the idea that life takes us into lots of different places or rooms. Some of these we like, some we do not like. Building positive images of these rooms and establishing what they might be for, how we can use them and if we need to continue with them, are the subjects of this chapter.

Most neurotypical people learn how to 'put on a face'. This is a metaphor. When I use these words I am using words I don't mean literally, to explain a concept. 'Putting on a face' means giving a facial expression for a particular event that might not be what the person really feels like doing. Some examples of this are: putting on a brave face (when a person feels scared), putting on a happy face (when a person feels sad) putting on a thankful face (when really a person feels disappointed). There is a list of metaphors and some general explanations toward the end of this book. These are to assist you in exploring their fuller meanings.

Chapter 4 (Covering the walls) explores the term 'putting on appearances'. It examines how neurotypical people use their theatrical imagination to build pictures of what they believe other people want from them. This is something we find difficult to understand, let alone do! However, to assist us it would be useful to gain an understanding of this concept as well as know when it would be good to employ it.

Most buildings need plumbing and electricity to operate efficiently. Chapter 5 (Plumbing and electricity) looks at what we, like everyone else, will need to give us power and efficiency as we dwell within our building. We will need to access amenities, nourish ourselves, keep ourselves warm and learn how to share our resources with others. It doesn't seem to be a good idea to live independently and believe that we will never need anything from anyone. This only isolates us and encourages other people to scorn us. What we need to do is to understand the concept of interdependence. We need to know this so that we can use the systems of life encounters more successfully.

We cannot choose the families we are born into nor can we always have the kind of control over outcomes that we would like to have.

Chapter 6 (Past influences upon how we build our lives) explores the various settings that life brings our way, whether it is via childhood education, teenage difficulties or employment issues. What career will suit me? What skills can I develop? How can I know what 'me' is and what do I do about the various crossroads and junctions I am challenged with?

Each building will have neighbouring buildings. Some neighbours live quite close to us, others will have long distances between themselves and their nearest neighbours. Chapter 7 (My building in relationship to my neighbours) looks at life as a journey that will involve others. Sometimes I wish that all the people would leave and let me get on with my life in the way I choose to live it! However, this isn't going to happen, therefore I need to explore what this might mean. For example, what is the best way to relate to others? Is there only one way? What does 'relating' mean? Most people seem to do many things at once. Will I be able to be like this? How can I fit my building into being the way I want it to be? Can I do this?

Chapter 8 (Buildings in need of maintenance and repair) suggests that all buildings need maintenance. Life is full of change and change can lead to things being done differently. Sometimes change can cause difficulties. Change for us can be very scary and we are usually not too keen on it. This chapter explores how neurotypicals cope with change, what they feel about it and what strategies they find helpful. It also looks at how we could use some of their strategies and why the repairing of damaged buildings is a good cost effective tool for the present and the future.

'Revisiting my plans and seeing where they lead me' is the title of Chapter 9. It is important to check in on our life travels from time to time. We could benefit from looking over our building, seeing how we have shaped who we are and how we can maintain who we want to be. We need to practise the things we learn in life or else we are in danger of losing them. It's a bit like the need to use our muscles in order to keep them strong.

Chapter 10 is the last chapter in this book; however, it is in no way a conclusion. Our journeys will be ongoing and always leading us into new places. In this chapter we explore how our journeys might lead us in different directions. We are all different individuals and we have our own particular characteristics, likes, dislikes, hopes and dreams. We need to find the appropriate map that suits our life journey, our lifestyle. We also need to learn how to use our maps and how to keep safe during the process.

Happy building, fellow traveller!

CHAPTER 1

Foundations for life

When I was a child I used to sing a song about a wise man who built his house upon the rock. When the storms came and beat upon that house it stood firm and didn't collapse. The song also mentioned a foolish man who built his house upon sand. When the storms came and beat upon his house it did collapse because the foundations for the house were not able to sustain it in a storm. How can we make sure that we build our house, ourselves, upon a firm foundation? What kinds of materials could we use? If we use negative self-concepts, criticism, defeatist viewpoints and 'poor me' scenarios like 'I'm no good at anything' then we are using the wrong materials for a strong foundation. These types of materials are all around us and it's tempting to pick them up and mix them into our lives.

What is the foundation for 'who you are' made of?

BRICKS AND CEMENT SOLID FOUNDATIONS

BROKEN STICKS AND RUBBISH ... WEAK FOUNDATIONS

I know at times I am very frustrated with the uneven skill profile that seems to dictate what I can and cannot do. For example, one of the things I love doing is watching insects and birds. I can watch them for hours. I don't have a problem giving this pastime my attention. The reason for this is that I am interested in birds and in insects. It's easy to give my attention to things of my interest. You might be able to say the same thing about things that interest you. However, it's very difficult for me to give my attention to things that don't interest me. For example, most other people and most other activities. This can cause conflict between others and myself.

It would be easy for other people to read my lack of attentiveness as rudeness, laziness, inability to share an interest or even sheer snobbery. However, actually it's my being 'attention tunnelled' or monotropic (Murray, 1992, see **page 22** of this text) and unable to have several other interests concurrent. Yes, this can be frustrating for us all. I can be so good at so many things that occupy my interest system, but not very good at all at things that don't interest me.

I believe this to be part of my uneven skill distribution. Neuro-typical individuals tend to have a more even skill distribution, therefore they can attend to many different things at the same time. They are also able to use divided attention and attend to lots of things at once. This is called polytropism (Murray, 1992, see **page 21** of this text). I have two choices concerning these facts. I can feel cross with them and with myself for being who I am, or I can accept my differences and use them constructively in my building. I choose the latter even though I acknowledge the frustration of the former.

Some of us might argue that we are not responsible for what goes into the foundations of who we are. After all, I am the product of my genes and upbringing. I understand that we did not choose the family line we were born into. My parents, grandparents and great grand-parents before them might have been given to a particular disposi-tion. This is true for us all. Some of us had parents who were outgoing, innovative, thoughtful, constructive and supportive. Others had parents who were critical, careless, defensive and non-supportive. Where does this lead? Well, it might lead to a genetic disposition for one or the other in us, but this is only a disposition, it is not the whole picture of who we are. We are also the sum of what we think and what we decide. We each make a huge contribution to the foundation of who we are, by our own choices. What will you choose to mix into the material of your building?

Neurotypicality and the spectrum of autism

The following is an attempt to demonstrate some of the differences in the ways neurotypical individuals, and individuals within the spectrum of autism are put together. In this description I am only writing about the cognitive processes that I believe help to construct understanding. To gain an overall picture, one must also consider individual personality, culture, age, gender, value systems and education. The processes outlined below might give you more understanding of individuals.

A description of the way neurotypical individuals process life: neurotypical (non-autistic) cognitive experience is informed by the following characteristics,

○ **Polytropism** or multi-channelling: (at the sensory level, using several channels simultaneously, eg. visual, auditory and spatial; at the cognitive level, having many interests simultaneously aroused). For example, can look at someone who is speaking whilst listening to them and being aware of the bigger world both within themselves and around themselves; can make multiple connections, identify context and scale, and easily model alternative possibilities and viewpoints.

○ **Non-literality**: understands incomplete sentences, incomplete concepts, metaphor and the non-literal 'sense' of everyday life. Reads a person's intention, the context and the scale of the event (over-all interpretation).

○ **Thinking in open pictures**: able to connect experiences, often visually, in an open and continuous manner. This process informs awareness, aids the understanding of social

cueing, helps with the sorting of priorities and
appropriateness.

○ **Social priorities**: for example, social norms, rules,
expectations and being sociable, are seen as priorities. Helps
with collating information about self, others and society. A
useful tool in social relating.

○ **Generalised learning**: having the ability to transfer skills
and knowledge across differing situations.

○ **Limited issue with time and motion**: can appreciate
length of time, timing and sequencing. Can negotiate stairs,
personal space, crowds and so on.

○ **Little issue with consequences**: is able to understand and
predict outcomes.

○ **Understands the concept of 'other'**: possesses a
well-developed 'theory of mind'.

Cognitive Processes informing the experience of being an individual on the autism spectrum

○ **Monotropism** or being singly channelled: (for example,
only able to focus on one thing at any one time, or only
comfortable with using one channel at any one time, such as
the visual channel). Looking at someone and listening to
them could be difficult. Consequently individuals with
autism/Asperger's may be perceived as being 'rude,' not
interested or not interesting. Can be a negative when it
comes to social relationships but very much a positive in the
world of 'concentration' on areas of one's interest.

○ **Literality** (or taking things literally): for example: sentences,
concepts, metaphor, simile, words, expressions, situations,
and people. May mean that it is difficult to 'read' intention,
context or scale.

○ **Thinking in closed pictures**: for example, not connecting
ideas or concepts. Not being privy to the 'whole picture' but

only getting bits of it can be rather limiting. Within a social context this makes it hard to 'read' others, anticipate their needs, be spontaneous, work or/and relate without schedules and refocus after being interrupted.

○ **Non-social priorities**: for example, preferred clothing versus fashion. This can cause a conflict of interest. Individuals with ASD may not be concerned with appearance, hygiene, being on time or having a tidy home. Or, on the contrary, they may be quite the opposite and will be regimented about these things to the point of distraction!

○ **Non-generalized learning**: this implies not transferring skills or knowledge. Even if an individual with ASD is abused, used or 'taken for granted', they may not learn from this and be wiser next time. Not generalising makes it difficult to differentiate between appropriateness and being inappropriate. For example, teaching that masturbation can occur in the bedroom or the toilet doesn't teach that an individual doesn't need to masturbate every time they go to their bedroom or use the toilet.

○ **Issues with time and motion**: this can mean problems with sequencing, timing and/or motor coordination. Within the realm of one's sexuality and/or relationships, this can mean social concepts such as being prompt, being organised, being apt, being appropriate in conversation and being generally coordinated are difficult.

○ **Issues with predicting outcomes**: for example, not learning from experience or being able to forward think and work out conclusions. This will mean missing social cues, not comprehending importance of 'special occasions', finding the idea of 'romance' interesting but not necessary, and so on.

○ **Issues with 'Theory of mind'**: (mis-understanding the concept of 'other'; empathy lacks and empathy gaps). I can be very sympathetic though, as long as you tell me that's what you need!

I believe that the differences outlined above are fundamental to the difficulties that you and I may experience. It might seem at times that we are aliens living in a world that just doesn't make much sense to us. We might even be tempted to give up trying!

Disability or differently abled?

Before exploring each of the points above, consider for a moment some of the words associated with autism. It is essential to good foundations that the ground we build upon be safe, reliable ground. How do you think of yourself?

The terms used to label us in our psychological assessments include the words 'disability' or 'disorder'. Let's look at these words. First, to explore the word 'dis-ability' we could take another 'dis' word, for example, 'dis-satisfaction. Taken logically and literally this might mean dis-ability becomes un-ability just as dis-satisfaction becomes un-satisfaction. How do you feel about being dis-abled? Do you feel dis-empowered by this word? Do you believe dis-satisfaction to be non-satisfaction and dis-ability to be non-ability? 'Well yes, Wendy, at times I do'. Yes, I know this experience too. However, let me just say that un-ability in some situations is quite different to being 'non-able'. The word 'non' suggests a total lack of ability. This just isn't true. We have plenty of ability! Unfortunately though we live in a world that might not be looking for our ability and, therefore, only sees our dis-ability. We can be partly responsible for helping this to change.

To place this further into context picture a visually impaired individual who has their necessary aids and supports (specific pre-scription lenses, white cane, seeing–eye dog, another individual) whilst moving around an unfamiliar supermarket. Now picture that same individual without their necessary supports moving around an unfamiliar supermarket. In one situation we would probably recognise their disability but view them as being quite able. In the other situation we might not 'see' their disability. We might perceive them as being non-able, and, as they bump into us, or other things, even see them as being a threat to our ability!

I suggest that the very word 'dis-ability' has social and medical constructs around it that need challenging. When our being autistic is seen in the context of our ability and not just our dis-ability, then we are moving in the right direction. In exploring the creation of a 'sighted' world we give the visually impaired individual the means to 'see' what is around them. This implies a lack of focusing upon their 'blindness' but rather on helping them see. So it is when one adapts the environment to fit us as individuals with ASD and provide us with the necessary maps for life navigation!

I would also suggest that being dis-abled is being differently able. A new term that someone introduced me to in the year 2002 was 'diffability'. Society would do well to accommodate and celebrate individual difference. To begin to do this, yes, one must accept and celebrate one's dis-ability. However, in that acceptance we would benefit from understanding both our limitations and non-limitations as ASD individuals. With the appropriate understanding, support and accommodation of our differing learning styles, those of us as individuals with ASD, and those with neurotypicality, have a better chance at cohabitation.

Autism is often referred to in the literature as 'a triad of impairments'. In describing autism it is said that we have impaired social understanding, impaired communication and impaired imagination, thus the 'triad of impairments'. To view autism as 'a triad of impairments' is like comparing us to an impaired washing machine that is 'out of order'! It doesn't receive signals, process information or complete a cycle. This is far too simplistic – autism is more a case of un-ability in some situations. I think that even neurotypicals find themselves dis-abled in certain unfamiliar and unrehearsed situations, too. I recently asked a large audience of people to respond to three statements. 'Put up your hand if you don't have any difficulties with social understanding,' 'Put up your hand if you don't have any difficulty with communication,' 'Put up your hand if you don't have any difficulty with aspects of imagination.' Not one person in this large group raised their hand! The triad of impairments seems to affect neurotypicals as well.

Words

Every thought I ever had was made of someone's words.
Every picture I can see, consists of words so perfectly.
In this understanding though, There is such a lot to know.
What if I get it wrong?

I thought I had the picture right,
I thought I had the words that night.
Then the person looked my way,
'What was it that you tried to say?'
They didn't know.

Why were they not listening?
Why didn't they understand?
To me it makes such utter sense,
Yet they just 'beat around the fence'.
I don't get it!

I use words to say exactly what I mean.
I use words to say only what is seen.
I use words to show where I have been.
I use words because they are a beam.
What do they show?

They tell us that we all think things,
They show and tell their act.
The difficulty here with words is obviously a fact.
You have your words and I have mine,
They may not be the same.
Please teach me what your words might mean,
And I will teach you mine.

Although our words describe for us the path our life road
takes.
They may lead to different maps,
They may produce big wide gaps,
What does your map show?

I want our words to cross over.
I want mine to meet with yours.
I want to come out from 'under cover'.
Can I trust you with my course?
Will you listen?

Thank you for saying you will.
Thank you for being here still.
You in your world and I in mine,
Together sharing some space.
Together we're building, this time.

I find my life much easier to handle when I consider that I have a diffability. If I view this as the foundation for all that I build, I feel happier with 'who' I am. I also think that coming from this perspective, I'm more likely to accept 'good building material' for the foundations of my life. When people criticise me and make inappropriate judgements about my abilities, behaviour or choices, I can be more forgiving of their ignorance and not take it personally. This means I am digging deep and firm confidence into the footings of my building. If, however, I accept their criticisms negatively, resenting them and choosing to 'close off' from them, then I am digging deep and firm 'low self-esteem' into the footings of my building. I have decided that I won't give this 'right' to anyone else, only to me. Other individuals may attempt to 'undermine my confidence' but I won't allow them that pleasure!

Home in Warrnambool

Recently we had an extension built onto the side of our home. When the builder inspected the ground to see how deep the footings needed to be, he also checked the ground for soil type. He wanted to make sure that the ground was firm enough to take the building. He also needed to check that the ground wasn't water logged or likely to subside. Having the right mix for the soil and being sure that the ground was firm enough to hold the extension was very important information.

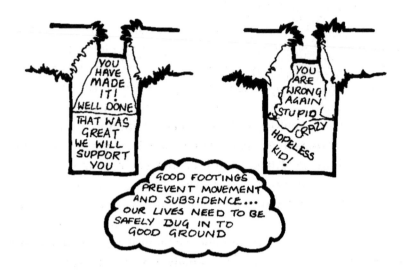

Building good footings for who I am

The footings for my life

When I decided to explore the 'soil' that the building of my life was/is erected upon I thought I would check to see if it was/is firm, safe from subsidence and strong enough to hold me for the rest of my life.

I also decided to check for any weeds that might be growing inappropriately. Weeds might be those words that people use that choke the life out of us. For example, words like 'lazy, incapable, dumb, dick head, silly, thick, stupid, crazy, mad, ridiculous, no good' and so on. I made up a solution of weed killer and I poured it over the ground. The ingredients of a good weed killer for inappropriate words consists of a solution of 'appropriate words'. I poured 'not interested' over 'lazy' and 'unmotivated' over 'incapable' and so on. I know when my interest is sparked I am highly motivated and work well.

Now that the groundwork is on its way, let's explore some of the processes that neurotypical individuals employ and compare them to how we process everyday life.

Polytropism in neurotypicality

When individuals can divide their attention and attend to a number
of different things at once, it makes it easier to take in multiple bits of
information from a number of different sources. For example, such
individuals can look at someone talking to them, listen to what they
are saying and process the content of that information whilst being
aware of the state of their bladder, their position in a room, time,
appropriate words they may need to use in any reply and also
understand when it's time to finish a conversation or start a new one.
Polytropic individuals are pretty adept at being multi-channelled.

This can be a useful tool in many situations that require multi-
channelling. However, it can get in the way a bit when they need to be
focussed and use attention for only one thing at any one time. It also
might present as an obstacle when individuals don't realise that not
all people are multi-channelled and they expect that everyone is.

This expectation is often passed on to us. I'm not too good at looking, listening and processing all at the same time. If I attempt this and fail, then I'm judged as 'not paying attention'. Not paying attention is a metaphor that implies 'You don't seem able to do this', 'you don't seem interested…you are hopeless' and so on. The truth is I am not 'able' in this situation because I am being asked to perform activities that I am not designed for. If the same activities were to be presented to me differently, connected to areas of my interest, one step at a time, in a programmed sequence, for instance, then I would probably be very 'able'.

We do better in social situations, for example, when conversation is clear, defined and when we know the rules. For example, what are the expectations of this conversation; how much time is there to talk; how much detail should we go into, and so on. I think we need to tell polytropic individuals that we need this. They are good at telling us what they need. Now it's our turn to tell them what we need. You might find it helpful to explain to someone talking to you that you need them to slow the conversation down a bit, not be in such a rush. They need to say what they mean clearly and give you time to think. It's perfectly fine to do this.

Monotropism

Many of us find that we have all of our attention in one place. We may only be interested in one topic at any one time. We may miss information that isn't connected to our attention and/or interest systems. This is a design feature of who we are. This is foundational to all other aspects of our building. It is very difficult to attend to information that is locked away from us, that we are not connected to. This is not a matter of being 'no-good' or of being lazy, it is simply not seen, not noticed, not attended to because all of our attention is taken up somewhere else. It's as if we are living our lives in one room of our building. When we need to, we can travel from that room into others. But, for us, this is always one room at any one time and we have our favourite room where we spend most of our time. If we tried to be in many rooms at once we would feel overloaded and extremely stretched! Polytropic individuals seem to be able to do this... they talk about 'having their finger in lots of pies' or of 'being everywhere at once' and so on. When I couldn't 'hold lots of different information in my head' and appeared to be very forgetful, people would say 'Wendy, you'd forget your head if it wasn't screwed on' or, 'think, Wendy'. Not only did I find their words difficult to interpret (there were no screws in my head; no-one told me what I was supposed to 'think' about) they were asking things of me that I couldn't do in the way that they expected. If I write a list, I can do what is asked. If I program my electronic organiser it can beep to remind me to look at it and then I know what to do next. We benefit from these types of tools just like business people need diaries, and take one appointment at one time.

Being non-literal

This means that most neurotypical individuals tend to understand non-literal meanings of words, sentences and so on, even when they are not 'spelled out'. For example, the intention, the context and the scale of what is being said or communicated is 'read', even if the words don't match the activity or no words are used at all. Here are some examples: 'pull your finger out' actually means 'work harder'; 'pull yourself together' actually is understood as 'don't be whatever it is you are feeling now, be in control of your emotions rather than allowing them to control you'; 'pull your weight' actually is meant to be read as 'please help us'. Sometimes individuals say words or tell us things that are quite difficult for us to appreciate because the code used is not understood or known by us. When we can 'break' the codes we are in a better position to access 'meaning' and then we can respond.

The factors to remember are that neurotypicals often don't finish their sentences (eg. they say they are going 'out' but don't say that they are coming 'in' again). It appears that a certain amount of information doesn't need to be said because it is 'understood' or 'assumed'. Quite a lot of metaphor is used in conversations between neurotypicals. For example 'the boss isn't himself' doesn't mean he has decided to become someone else. It means that the boss's behaviour is out of character for him...possibly he is unwell or feeling sad and this means he isn't his 'usual' self. It will also mean that if you are told this, there is an expectation upon your behaviour too. This might mean that you are expected to be less demanding of the boss's time, be kind to them or simply forgive the boss if he/she isn't nice to you.

Neurotypical individuals say things to each other without using words at times. They might use gesture, facial expressions and/or other body language to get their point over (say what they mean without words). Sometimes this means changing the arrangement of their eyebrows, mouths, arms, legs and so on. For example, when a person's eye brows are pointing up at the far end and down towards their noses, they are probably feeling cross and are trying to tell you this with their faces. If we are not attending to this detail, however, we might miss this information and not realise that this is how they feel.

Literality

Unlike neurotypical people we are often very literal. We may find metaphors helpful, as long as we clearly understand them, as in this book. We like to say what we mean, say what we think and say what we understand needs to be said. I value verbal expression much more than visual or bodily expression because it is far easier to understand.

However, if those talking to me are not clear with the language they use and cloak their words in codes of 'subtle body language without words', I might misread them. If you mean 'please help me', don't say 'pull your weight'! If I don't understand and the neurotypical individual judges my behaviour as inappropriate, they might call me a word which isn't helpful to my self-esteem. This could become a weed in the foundations of my building. I need to try to prevent this by letting the person know that I wasn't being unhelpful, I just wasn't sure of what was wanted from me. I can say to that person 'Please tell me what you need from me'. This way we can both be talking the same language without the need for any decoding.

Thinking in open pictures

Polytropic individuals are often very good at having visual thoughts that are connected with other thoughts, emotions and possible responses. When speaking to a group of people, I sometimes ask them to close their eyes for a few seconds and think about the word 'home'. Then I tell them to open their eyes and report to the rest of us what it was they 'saw'. Usually people say things like 'my sitting room'; 'the family at dinner'; 'the fire'; 'the washing-up', 'peace'; 'chaos'; 'my garden'; 'the cat'. As you will notice, the word 'peace' is 'seen' by some. This word represents an emotional state...the lack of turmoil. How can one visualise such a feeling? How can individuals wander around an environment within their minds, connecting rooms of their home to activities they do there and emotions they feel? This is what it means to think in open pictures. It means the ability to connect many aspects of different environments in a visual and ongoing manner.

Thinking in closed pictures

I too am a 'visual' person. I don't have any difficulties with thinking of things and seeing their visual representation. However, I do have difficulty in linking this information together, interpreting and generalising it. When it comes to specific types of information that are linked to areas of my interest, I can easily attend to them and then I don't have this problem. I think this occurs because the information

Attention tunnel

is within my attention tunnel, not outside of it. I already have the facts
in order to be able to place the pieces together to form a 'constant' or a
set model. It is adapting this, thinking in the future of 'what if' that
really presents a problem for me. This is the main reason that I find
change difficult. I'm uncomfortable because I'm not sure what
'change' will mean.

Autism and transition

Autism is: 'I like it here, please do let me stay'.
Autism is: 'I know it here, please don't take me away'.
If and when I leave this place to travel to another space,
I need to know it right away. I need to know that I'm OK.
Transition is so fleeting, it leaves not time to stay.
Will I have time to settle, or will I be whisked away?

I know that change can happen.
I know it can take time.
But how can I know what this will mean?
What this will mean for mine.

Transition is about moving, 'to where or what' one asks?
This is my very question, from present or the past.
Time for me is all the same,
I know not of its future.
I only know I trust in 'now'... tomorrow can come, I just
need to know how.

Transition is an amazing part of everyday life. It is so common that
many people will hardly notice it: moving from sleeping to waking;
from night to day; from nightclothes to day clothes; from home to car
and so on. Major transitions, like pre-school to primary school;
primary school to secondary school; school to employment; family
home to setting up own home; marriage; children; middle age and so
on are much more noticeable.

In autism, the minor transitions of everyday life can be extremely
traumatic. Transition and autism are like enemies. They are foreign to
one another because they represent opposing abilities. Transition says
'It's time to move on', and assumes one is ready, able and willing.
Autism says 'I have to stay here because here is all I know'. It assumes
that outside of 'here', there is *chaos, confusion and conflict*. In order for
any transition to 'go well' or even just be tolerated we have to have the
three C's we just mentioned (chaos, confusion and conflict) sorted
into *order, understanding and calm.*

Change

Change, change and more change,
Of context, place and time.
Why is it that Life's transient stage
Plays havoc with my mind?

You said, 'We'll go to McDonald's'
But this was just a thought.
I was set for hours,
But the plan then came to naught.

My tears and confused frustration,
At plans that do not appear,
Are painful beyond recognition,
And push me deeper into fear.

How can life be so determined?
How can change be so complete?
With continuity there is no end,
Security and trust are sweet.

So, who said that change would not hurt me?
Who said my 'being' could not be safe?
Change said, 'You need continuity'
In order to find your place.

For change makes all things different,
They no longer are the same.
What was it that you really meant?
All I feel is the pain.

Lawson, 2001

Misunderstanding adds to the stress we each experience. For any transition to occur effectively, we all need to feel safe and assured.

Sometimes transition is difficult to encounter or process because the *concept* is too overwhelming. It's all too much to take in… remember, being monotropic will mean we can only focus on one thing at any one time. Being autistic will mean that we process information in 'bits' and not in 'reams'. If I am presented with too much information I'll switch off, go into overload or just not be very nice! This is because being overloaded is uncomfortable and causes me pain. I find it helpful to recognise this happening and let the person know, so that I can take care of myself and of their feelings.

Over time life demands different things of us at different times. This is OK, as long as we understand what those demands might mean for us and for others.

In the pub?

Revelation (The process of growing-up)

I use to be much smaller but now I am much taller.
I use to stride my walker but now I am a talker.
Skipping rope was what I liked but that was before I got my bike.
My dog Rusty loved to swim, without warning she'd jump right in!
My sisters use to tease me bad, so when I could I teased them back.
I use to think to smoke was cool, but now I know I was a fool.
To be a nurse would be unreal, is what I used to always feel.
Now I want to know much more and see what lies through a different door.
So I can tell, from these few words, that as I grow and get to know just who
I am and why I came, I may not need to stay the same.

Social priorities

Neurotypical individuals who are polytropic and able to form links to lots of information which can then be revisited, generalised and used appropriately, have the advantage in social situations. When I am relating to another individual, one to one, and we are sharing some mutual interest or goal, I believe my communication can be very good. However, when I am in situations that require multi-processing of multi-information and possibly impacted by a range of other sensory issues (people, noises, distraction) then communication can be very difficult, frustrating and even misleading.

Being able to prioritise, organise and strategise requires clear thinking, functional organisational ability, propriety and motivation. All of these skills I possess but only in specific situations. My diffability will mean that multi-processing will be difficult and very taxing. My head can physically 'ache' with the strain of trying to work out what I need to do. When situations are clearly defined, physically, emotionally and with my role spelled out, I can often cope. Social priorities are not a large part of what motivates me, nor do I understand why they are so highly valued amongst the polytropic populace. However, they seem to possess a real importance for this group and I need to respect that. Therefore, I need to work out 'my place' in it all and 'their place', so we are both kept happy.

Being focussed and not appreciating generalised concepts

Generalising

This is the process that requires us all to practice specific skills, knowledge and/or social understanding in a variety of situations and circumstances. Most of the time we don't even realise that this is what is happening. If, however, you are like me you might find this process rather tiring.

I am pretty good at learning a whole range of things. For example, riding a bicycle, roller skating, dog training and cooking. However, I'm not so good at generalising some of the concepts needed in these activities. This might mean that skills needed for skating (e.g. looking where I am going; not getting distracted by others and so on) might not generalise to other activities such as the skills that might be needed when in a large shopping complex. I also noted that I only skated in one location, only rode my bike at specific times and on certain roads, only trained my own dog and only enjoyed cooking the same meals that I always cooked!

Using knowledge generalised to apply to lots of different situations, occasions and interactions is difficult for us because we are monotropic and tend to think in closed pictures. This might mean that we miss the point of some interactions, only focussing on the immediate, apparent and/or literal. If our thinking is in a closed visual forum then we might not be able to access the links that polytropic individuals take for granted. I think this is one reason we tend to be negative about ourselves. It is much easier for us to 'believe' people who are critical of us and add their words, like weeds, to our footings because we see only the reality of our failings. I hope this book will help you to see beyond such occasions, forgive their ignorance and only accept words that strengthen the ground for you.

Issues with time

I don't know about you, but time for me is a very difficult concept to understand. I'm good at telling the time, by reading the time from a watch or a clock, but I'm not so good at knowing how much time has elapsed; how much time I need to give to an event; what 'timing' is all about and/or what other people's concept of time is.

This can present lots of potential problems for us. I remember on my school reports that I was said to 'take too much time to...' Well, how much time is 'too much time'? I often arrive far too early for an event because I am so anxious about being late. I am easily pre-occupied by 'time' and I need to check the time often. I get upset with other people when they don't seem to observe the same rules as I do, concerning time. Sometimes someone has said to me 'I'll ring you and let you know'. This has meant, for me, sitting near the telephone waiting for it to ring! Usually, I now understand that the person will ring when they can. I don't need to sit near the phone and wait for the call. I am allowed to do other things. If their call comes when I am busy, I can let the answer machine take it. I used to say 'yes' to almost anything. It got me into less trouble than saying 'no'. Now, I'm trying to revisit this and allow myself the room to gain 'time' to think about it before I answer. We are allowed to do this.

Being kind to myself, to others and trying not to get too upset about 'timing' is putting good material into the foundations of my building. I know it's hard to get the balance between making the most of one's 'time', postponing time and taking time out for needed space. It's perfectly OK to take your time with this one!

Forward thinking and consequences

So many times someone would say to me 'You're so scatty, Wendy'. This type of comment isn't very helpful! Being able to 'forward think' and predict outcomes is hard for us because we are monotropic and, therefore, only able to attend to one thing at one time, the 'now'. I am not good at 'seeing' where my actions, words or ideas might lead me. I accept this and I have found it very useful to check things out with a good friend who knows and accepts me. Choosing the right person to relate to isn't easy, but it is very important. We are good people to have as friends. We are loyal, truthful, honest and dependable. Sometimes people don't see our good qualities. This is their loss, not ours. When you are locating possible individuals to add to your circle of friends, check them out first. We all need stable, dependable relationships. If the person you want to have as a friend doesn't fit this description, they may not be good friend material. Another definite contribution to potential friendship is that the person wants to be your friend!

Because of the difficulty that so many of us have with issues connecting to 'time', I think that making lists and/or having a diary can be very useful. You might like a paperback or hardback diary; you may, like me, prefer an electronic diary or organiser. I can program my organiser in a sequential fashion for any particular day and it will then 'beep' to prompt me to look at it and 'see' what the next event of my day will be. Due to my difficulties with time I find it hard to organise my time, therefore, organisers are very helpful. I know it's not always easy to accept our limitations. I know that limitations are different for each of us. However, I have found that 'coming to terms' with my limitations has been very good. If I could name one component that I think is essential in the foundation of my building, it is this one. I don't 'use' my limitations as an excuse for not doing things I probably could do, but I do accept the things I can't do and allow others to support me, as they are able.

Key Points

- Being monotropic is the way I am designed (attention all in one place).

- Non-autistic people are polytropic (they simultaneously attend to many different things, e.g. thoughts, discourse, emotions, self, other).

- Building a good foundation for my life will mean I am choosy about what goes into it.

- I pour only worthwhile material into my foundation.

- I accept my diffability.

- I am my building.

CHAPTER 2

Designing, planning and structuring our building

Being supported whilst we build who we are

Scaffolding

Now that we have considered laying good foundations for our building (secure footings of self-acceptance, including limitations; soil rich in firmness, tolerance, patience with self and other) all cemented with ability, determination and strength of character, we can erect the scaffolding to support us for the rest of our building. For us, in this book, scaffolding will represent the framework in which we develop. It will also refer to the support we need from other people, agencies and/or ourselves.

In different places around the world I have noticed that differing scaffolding techniques seem to apply. For example, in England I saw brick walls being built upon concrete foundations. The skeletal scaffolding system seemed to go up with the walls, one at a time. In other places I noticed that scaffolding can be built up first, then the wooden framework and last, the walls. I don't know why it's different for different places and perhaps it doesn't matter. The important thing is, though, that every building, during construction (unless prefabricated, maybe) requires scaffolding. Scaffolding is a skeleton of poles and planks that is erected around the building during its development. In order for it to be good scaffolding several points need consideration. For example, it must be strong, safe, adequate and appropriate. If our building is three storeys high, then scaffolding for a two-storey building might be strong and safe, but it won't be adequate or appropriate! A potential three-storey building requires scaffolding for a three-storey building.

Our building

We all develop over time. We start out as babies, become children, teenagers and eventually adults. The support needs for a baby are different from those needed for most older children and different again for teenagers and adults. When we were babies there may have been a time when it was perfectly OK to require and access parental/primary caregiver attention twenty-four hours a day. As we grew this diminished somewhat, and our caregivers hoped that we would sleep through the night and allow them to sleep too. By the time we were ourselves adults, most of us would get into trouble if we woke someone up to get their attention for our needs! Many of those needs that once involved others have changed. We are able to do lots of things on our own that don't require the help of others. In many ways we are more independent and more capable. Sometimes I hear speakers talking about developing independence. In fact, most of us know how to be independent in lots of ways but we have problems with being *inter-dependent*. We all need support in life. It is OK to need other people in our lives.

How can we work out what our building needs are? This is very important because this understanding will also define our scaffolding needs (our support needs). Well, I guess that the first step is to reassess your situation, as it exists today. We can't really go back in time and change where we have lived in our previous building of who we are. We need to consider things as we find them now.

Building requirements

You might like to draw up a chart. You could use an A4 exercise book, or just a piece of paper. You might like to refer to this often, though, to check out how you are doing. So, it's a good idea to be able to keep your book or sheet of paper safe, and in a place where you can easily find it again, if you need to. Down the centre of the page draw a line that divides one side from the other. Then, at the top of the page write the words 'building requirements'. Under this general heading write the word 'needs' on the left-hand side and 'wants' on the right hand side.

Under the word 'needs' make a list of what you think are essential things to have in your building, for example, rooms, doors, windows, power sockets, plumbing, and so on (see below). On the right side of your paper, under the word 'wants', you could list the things you would like to have; for example, non-essential things. Once your lists are ready, then you can consider the types of scaffolding or support you might need to help move you towards furnishing your needs and your wants.

This next section explores ideas about needs and wants to help with your chart.

Needs (e.g. rooms, windows, furniture, light and warmth)

How many rooms would you like in your building? Rooms can represent areas of your life that you 'live' in. You may have an 'everyday' room; an eating room; a work room; a family room; a bedroom; a room to cook in; a wash room, and a guest room. You know best what your needs are. Let's begin by looking at what you might like in your everyday room. Other terms for this room could be 'lounge' or 'living room'. In this room you need to feel comfy, warm, safe and welcome. In this room you can relax, feel refreshed and rebuild the energy systems that enable you to move to other rooms if you wish.

How big would you like your building to be? Do you see yourself as a skyscraper or a one bedroomed apartment? There aren't any rules here. You can be whichever one appeals to you the most! The important thing to remember is that you are comfortable with the outcome, can access the resources you need for this venture and can see yourself 'at home' with the idea. Sometimes it's better to start out small and give yourself room to develop and grow, rather than think too big and not be able to complete the project. You are in control of this, so you can make the decision.

I think it is important to consider needs and wants and realise the differences, yes. However, the paragraph below illustrates that sometimes my wants and my needs get muddled. Its best to start out accepting the basic design of who I am. I might not like 'me' and want to be someone else. However' acceptance of self is a need if I am to continue with building my life successfully.

Do you like the person you are? If you could change anything about yourself, what would it be? Some things it might be possible to change, other things might be established and would require too much to demolish. For example, I am trying (constantly) to control my weight. I don't like being overweight and I know my knee joints don't like it either. This is a process I can consent to or reject. It's pretty much up to me. However, the shape of my body is outside of my control, just as is my height, my freckles and my poor eyesight. I need to accept these as part of who I am. I need to pour my energy into constructing my building, not waste it upon ideas that can never be (for example, I cannot become a small boned woman without freckles who is good with numbers, but I can build towards being a lower weighted female developing better communication skills).

In considering my needs and wants it would be wise to appreciate that others have needs and wants too. Their needs and wants may be different to mine. However, we will each have dealings with others.

This will mean we need to consider their needs and wants, as well as we consider ours. Other people have 'rights'. They have the right to have their needs and wants considered. Negotiating this can be difficult, but not impossible. The trick is to aim at not upsetting others whilst we take care of ourselves in the process. I believe that I am a worthwhile person and other people are worthwhile too. I believe I am entitled to and have rights to healthy and profitable attitudes, memories and experiences. This goes for you and others too. These are the rights of all human beings. I know that not everyone can access these rights and there are many who can, but choose not to. Wants and needs exist in us all. Some people find it difficult to decide between these. Some do not consider others. Some choose to hold on to the rubbish in their lives (bad attiudes; hurtful behaviour). Unfortunately this is their right, the right to reject good things and keep only garbage in their building. I like the smell of good things more than the smell of rubbish, how about you? I choose to consider my needs and the needs of others.

Pongy rubbish V nice smelling flowers

Wants (desires, likes, extras)

Life might be very boring if all we got from it were the things we needed! At times I want something, not because I need it but because I desire it. Quite often this want is satisfied and quite legitimately so. For example, I want an ice cream while I watch a movie; I want to finish off a meal with a cup of sweet tea; I want to talk to a good friend; I want to run my hands across my cat's fur, and so on. Then, there are those times when my 'wants' are illegitimate (getting what I want might hurt someone else) or it's not my turn to have what I want. I am still learning that what I feel inside isn't always the whole story. This can be very confusing I know, especially when it doesn't seem that there is any more to the story. For this reason I am learning to listen to the wisdom of others that I trust. If they tell me 'there is more to this, Wendy', then I need to hear them.

Structuring wants

o   Check out if the feeling or thought belongs to a need or a want? Which one is it?

o   Will my satisfying this 'want' be within my financial limits for the week?

o   Will my having this 'want' upset anyone else?

o   Is it useful and legitimate for me to have this 'want' satisfied?

o   If I am not sure of any of the above then I may benefit from talking to my good friend about my wants and listen to his or her opinion.

o   I may have to put my 'wants' to one side and explore them again later.

Building Plans

Once you have made your lists of 'needs' and 'wants', have thought about the scaffolding you might need to help get you there (finances; other people; education; travel; moving house), and now must consider the actual construction of those things, it's time to draw up the plans. I found that I needed to share my lists with a good friend. A good friend is someone who chooses to be with and support you. They are happy to be involved with you and can be a bit objective in this whole process. My friend(s) helped me to explore what I needed and be realistic about my plans. They then also helped me to explore how I might go about drawing up the plans for the building of my life. At times, my good friend would point out that perhaps I wanted too much and might find it easier to concentrate more on my needs, as opposed to my wants. It was explained to me that 'wants' are often not necessities and should be considered as 'extras' to my requirements. This is not to say that I couldn't have them, just that they might not be an immediate priority. In fact, setting priorities was one of the things my good friend helped me with the most.

Building Friendship

Because I share quite intimate information about myself with my good friend I need to be sure that I can trust him or her. This is very important. Sometimes it is tempting to share all sorts of things that happen to us, but I try to check out first that the information I want to share is appropriate for this time, this place and this person. This can be difficult I know. I think it is helpful to ask yourself some questions before you share your life story with another. For example:

○ What is the nature of this information? (E.g. is it personal; intimate; for general release; for family only; superficial; deeply moving; fun; tragic and so on.)

○ Whose ears is this information for? (E.g. 'personal' means only good friends/family perhaps; 'intimate' might mean only your partner or possibly a very close friend; 'superficial' might mean you can tell all sorts of different people, as long as they are interested. You might need to ask them first if they want to hear what you have to say.

○ When/where should I tell? (E.g. at work; in the café; on the bus home.) Usually personal and intimate information needs to be shared in a private place and in confidence.

If you think after asking yourself the above questions that you are sure of what to share and with whom, then go ahead and tell them. If you need some feedback from them, you might need to reassure them of your need for their response. If you feel that their feedback is critical or unfair then tell them how you feel and ask if what they are saying could be presented in a more positive light. If, after revisiting this with them, you still feel uncomfortable, you might need to check it out further. I found that this was very useful to me. I also found that email and chat lists could be helpful, but you need to be sure that they are reputable, which can be difficult to assess.

Plans for the living room

This will mean that your living room must have sufficient light, heat, comfortable furnishings and be the right size for you. Essentially your living room is the main part of who you are. Are you comfortable with yourself? Can you take time to 'centre yourself', close the door upon demand, say 'no' to expectation and just allow yourself to retreat into the safety of your building?

We are easily overloaded by daily living demands. When our 'living room' is unsupported (because we lack the right scaffolding), it might be in danger of collapsing. The right scaffolding is one that gives us support when we need 'space' and quietness. It is OK to tell other individuals in your life that you need this. If you have to share your living room with others then your space and time might need some negotiating so that the living room can accommodate your needs and the needs of others.

As we know our building will have many different rooms. Each room has a function or purpose. Over time we will discover which rooms we feel comfortable in and which rooms we want to avoid. Some rooms are just for entertaining visitors in, some are closed to the public and others are for keeping things safe in. In other words you can choose what you share of yourself and what you keep private; what you allow others to access and what you keep just for you!

Support rules

You can have rules for your plans and structures if you like. The structures you need may be made from the support of others as well as the support from yourself. This might mean that you let other people know your living room needs (comfort, warmth, relaxation). It might mean that you need to be firm with others and/or with yourself so that you keep out noise, discomfort, coldness, inappropriate behaviour and/or demand. You might even need to request from your scaffolding (supporters) that conversation and action be constructive, enlightening, reassuring and rejuvenating. This will mean that any negative action or conversation can be kept out. You might even want to make a big sign for your living room door saying 'No Entry to Negativity'. If you do this, what might it mean if you feel a bit depressed, lost or down in your living room? Are these things negative and forbidden? No, definitely not! Being and feeling 'low' isn't negative, it's a statement of life in your living room for you, some of the time. It is the way you feel, it is not the total of who you are. The negative side of life is when you feel criticised, put down, made to feel unimportant and silly. This is the kind of inappropriate 'stuff' we want to keep out of our living rooms!

If you feel depressed or sad it is important to recognise the emotions you feel and welcome them. You might like to talk to yourself safely within your living room and even give yourself a gentle hug. You might like to share your feelings with those who support you and accept a hug or appropriate support from them. Acceptance of all of our emotions is important. Then we can sift through them, locate any action needed and even move on from them. Emotions are fickle things that change like the wind. You may never know for sure what direction they will take you in. This is OK. Many other people feel as you do. The important thing to remember, though, is that emotions are only one part of who you are. They don't need to control you because you are bigger than they are and you can take control of them. You might need some scaffolding to support you in this process, but you can do it.

Window size

Within the wall of your living room you might like a window. Windows allow us to look out over the world around us. Sometimes, they allow others to look in at us. You can decide what you will allow to be seen through your window. You can decide what you will show to yourself and what you will show to others. You might like to use blinds or curtains that allow you to cover your window. This might be important to you. Perhaps you need privacy sometimes? Perhaps you want to explore the world around you from the safety of your room? Shades for your window will let you choose what you share and what you keep safe for your eyes only.

Sometimes we don't know what we are allowed to look at and what we are to share with others. When I was a child I spoke with anyone and shared with everyone. This wasn't the best idea and it often got me into trouble. Now, I am wiser and I take more care of myself. I am allowed to choose not to show others the things that belong to me. I am also allowed to choose to share, if I wish. This will be the same for you.

I think it is important to welcome good thoughts and images into our living room. You can usually tell which thoughts and images are good because they make you feel good. I know it can be difficult at times. I like science fiction (Star Trek; Star Wars and such like). Some films on television are dramatised or use suspense to keep their audience mystified and entertained. I like watching such movies and TV shows, but I try not to watch them before I go to bed. I find that watching these types of shows may hinder my ability to relax and settle to sleep. I can usually video record these types of shows and then I am free to watch them at a future time when my sleep won't be disturbed. I love using the Internet. This is another area that can be used to let images and words into my living room that might be potentially disastrous for me, or you. I sometimes find it difficult to separate reality from fantasy. This means that I tend to take other people literally and do not always realise that they are joking or using metaphor. I can check this out by asking a neurotypical person, who I trust, what their opinion of the situation is. You could do the same.

I like to have comfortable and practical furniture in my rooms. One could think of relationships this way too. I find it best not to let other people drag me down and cause me discomfort. I know I have experienced times when I cannot control what another person says or does. However, I can control what I do. So, if they say or do things that upset me, I choose to give myself time to resolve this discomfort. It might be that I need to use 'the Weedkiller' mix, pouring positive, helpful and constructive words over their disruptive ones. At times I need to do this alone and to myself. At other times I need to do this publicly. I have found at such times, a letter is a good idea. Writing what one feels or thinks can be easier than saying it face to face. If I am finding that a relationship with a friend, neighbour or workmate is becoming uncomfortable, then I give myself some time to process my discomfort and sort it out.

Telling others how you feel or what you think won't always mean that they agree with you and are pleased with you. Sometimes they won't be and that is their decision. I cannot always make everyone happy and you won't be able to either. Their happiness, contentment and comfort might be in their own hands and not in ours. Having said this, I know at times I am the cause of another's discomfort and I need to explore how I can make them more comfortable. For example, at times I know I talk too much. So, I need to accept that there is a possibility others might be irritated by my constant chatter. Maybe they need a break from my talking. I don't like being told to stop talking, but I'm getting better at coping with this.

Further design or planning needs

I know that I am pretty good at knowing what programs I like to watch on TV, what food I like to eat for dinner and which items of clothing I like best to wear. However, when it comes to a wide range of other things (what I think about something; where I might like to go; what I need to say in a conversation and other decision/problem solving issues) I have great difficulty in responding quickly enough. At times I just cannot locate the information I am being asked for. At other times I can, but I take too long and by the time I get there the other person has moved along in the conversation. If you are like me you can perhaps identify with this. I think for us, it's fine to tell the person talking that we find this difficult. We might need their support to assist us with some areas of problem solving.

For example, I need support with getting myself organised. I have a diary, which I can write appointments in, but I often leave out vital information. I know this information at the time and don't remember that I might forget it when I put the phone down or get caught up in some other task. Therefore, it can be a good idea to write sections in your daily planner that prompt you to write things such as *name, address, phone number, date, time, activity* and so on. If we can take some time to rule these sections up, then the words are there ready for us to make use of when we need them. I also gain the support of my friends who are happy to remind me of events, activities and so on. I love to write down the things I need to remember to do, in lists.

Routine

I feel your presence inside of me,
I hear your voice when you ask to see.
But which is which and what is what?
I did remember, and then forgot.

I think I need this very thing,
But how can I know for sure?
Is it really what I need?
Should I ask for more?

More information, more advice?
Do I need a bigger slice?
Do I need it?
Do I want it?
Is it really worth the price?

Most of the time I cannot tell.
How do others know so well?
I think I'll pass on this small choice,
I think I'll find a bigger voice.

A voice of definites; absolutes and all.
A voice that is never small or tall.
A voice that says there's much and more.
A voice that I can trust for sure,
Routine.

Plans gone wrong

Routine, order and knowing what comes next are very important. Sometimes our plans don't seem to go the way we had hoped and this causes us distress. Having 'back-up' plans or 'plan B' as well as 'plan A', is a good idea. In any building process there seem to be things that don't always go according to The Plans! Usually, this is OK. It's all right when deviations happen along the way, as long as we have allowed for it. If you think of your plans and ideas, maybe you might 'change' your mind, or add something extra or take something away? This is your building, you are allowed to do this. If other people change their minds and after offering you the support you wanted, withdraw their support, this is something you need to accept. It won't be comfortable for either of you, but it is OK. Our building does not have to stop, our dreams do not have to die, we just have to find more support. Scaffolding for our needs and wants has to be adjustable. Maybe you know of particular support groups for ASD/AS? Maybe you know of particular agencies that are set up to give assistance in various ways to others? If you don't know of these, perhaps you might like to check with your local telephone directory under the heading of 'Services and Community'. There might be some useful telephone numbers there that you could use to see what other types of support you could find to help you.

Key Points

- Scaffolding goes up so that the building can safely be constructed.

- You can design your building. What will you put into it? How do you see yourself?

- What are your needs?

- What are your wants?

- Choose only the best materials for your building.

- Are your friends made from the best material? Check them out.

- How many rooms does your building have? What is your favourite room?

- It is important to know what we should or should not share with others. Some rooms are private, others are more public.

- Some rooms should not be entered, they may be dangerous. Others can be for storage and for visiting.

CHAPTER 3

Erecting the building

When I was younger I loved to explore the world outside. I wasn't very good at staying 'inside' and wanted to be out in the air, in the weather, in the uncontained spaces that held so many wondrous things to see and do. I would wander around streets, lanes, fields, woods and beaches, looking for excitement. I usually found it in the form of leaves, insects, animals, birds and flowers. There is so much 'life' out there! I still enjoy these things very much, but now my wanderings tend to be timetabled!

Diffability

Discovering about ourselves, our hopes, dreams, likes and dislikes, can be quite a journey. It's fine to take our time to do this. All the uncertainty and difficulty that we encounter are part of the process of discovery. Sometimes, when others comment on my choice of TV program, reading material, topic of conversation, choice of menu, likes, dislikes and so on, I doubt myself and am tempted to think of myself as some bizarre person who must be very strange. This is not the case! Being different, having different interests from others, is not strange. It might be difficult for some people to understand me, and you, but this is their problem, not ours.

Protection against the storms

Erecting rooms, like the living room in the previous chapter, might need some support from us, and from others, but it is still our room. Where I am comfortable, where you are comfortable, is your decision. We have the right to our choice of room, what we do there and whom we admit to this room. The only rules are that we treat ourselves, and others, with respect. If my room becomes untidy or needs some maintenance, then I see to it. My room can become what I want and/or need it to be. It should be safe, carefully constructed and weatherproof.

Me against the storms

Sometimes life can churn up some severe storms and gales. We need to keep these from intruding into our building. If, however, some elements of life's storms do make it past the walls and roof of our building, we can try to be ready for them.

As I wrote the words above a friend was sending me an email. Apparently some drain cleaning fluid that she had poured down into the drain via the bath had caused some damage to a fitting and the end result was three flooded rooms below! The email ended with bother, bother, bother! This is life sometimes and being able to say 'bother' is OK. I know it will mean calling in some help from an expert and financial costs, as well as hours of putting in the time to clear up the mess. But, it can be done. If this were happening to you or me we would feel very uncomfortable, frustrated and even cross. These emotions are OK to feel. However, they don't need to immobilise us. I can remember my mother telling me to 'Wipe up that mess, Wendy'. I replied, 'I can't. It's too wet'. My mother explained to me that actually I could wipe it up if I followed the right procedure. First I needed to dampen a cloth; then I needed to place that cloth over the spill; then I needed to lift the cloth carefully, not allowing its contents to pass through my fingers; then I needed to rinse the cloth and repeat the process until all of the spill was transferred from the floor into the sink and washed away.

I guess I'm saying that we might not always know what the right procedure is and this is OK. However, the best way to find out is to share our concerns with appropriate people and seek their assistance. What you and I need in our rooms are ways to erect safe, ordered and calm spaces that we can complete our activities in without fear.

Insulation

When you look at the plans you have made for the building of your life, it should tell you what rooms you hope to build, what their purpose is and what materials you will need in order to build them. We already know that materials must be strong, suitable and the best ones for the job. But, do we need any other materials? What about materials that go in between the rooms?

My home in Warrnambool

When the extension to our house was under construction we needed to decide what kind of insulation we were going to put within the roof space, above the ceilings and in between the walls. We wanted our rooms to be warm and also to be protected from too much noise that might infiltrate from room to room. I like quietness. I don't find it easy to concentrate on my activities if noise is distracting me. Therefore, we chose two types of insulation. One was typical 'insulation batts' of 1.5, the other was called 'acoustic batts'. The usual 1.5 'batts' provided insulation and would help to keep our rooms warm in winter and cooler in summer. The acoustic batts would help to reduce the transference of noise from room to room.

During the building of your life with its various rooms you might need to consider what your insulation needs are. Insulation needs could translate to personal relationships. What kind of relationships do you currently have? Are they relationships that keep you warm? Do they clutter up your building and make life too noisy for you? Are the people in your life causing you to prosper, develop and mature? Or, do they make you feel small, unimportant and unmotivated? I think it is important to have friends and family in my life. However, I hope that my friends and family can relate to me in an atmosphere of acceptance and of mutuality.

There was a time in my life when I seemed to attract only injured or damaged individuals who needed me for their own problems. I was quickly drained of life and couldn't find any spare, warm rooms to retreat into for myself. Every one of my rooms was occupied by needy others. Now it is fine to have friends who are sometimes needy; we are all needy at some time or another. However, it is important to keep space for yourself and to have people in your life who nourish who you are. Self-acceptance is not much good if we are the only ones who accept ourselves. We need acceptance from others too.

Most of us need to share with another person, from time to time. During a conversation with a good friend I can share ideas, hopes, thoughts and desires. I can also listen to my friend as he or she shares this sort of thing with me. This mutual exchange makes me feel good and offers great insulation against the coldness of some of life's daily encounters.

Dreams, hopes and achievements

Dreams, hopes and achievements are very positive types of rooms that we all need in our building. They coexist with everyday rooms and utility rooms.

What does your room of dreams look like? Dreams are the pictures we have in our heads, sometimes whilst we are sleeping and sometimes when we are still awake. On the television, sometimes, there is an advertisement which says 'Don't just dream it, do it!' Well, it is OK to dream and keep your pictures as dreams. You don't always need to convert your dreams and make them a reality. It is also OK to consider turning your dreams into achievement. How you tell which ones you want to keep as dreams and which ones you want to make real might be a challenge, but it is a challenge worth considering.

Questions/Guidelines for converting dreams

- Do you want this dream to become a reality?

- What would it take to make it a reality? For example, I wanted to go to University, but I didn't qualify. The first step was to go back to school, do years 11 and 12, get the qualifications I needed, then apply for university.

- Could you do this on your own, or will you need help?

- What kind of help would you need? Help from others? Financial help? Material help? Organisational help?

- Are you willing to elicit appropriate support?

- Would you rather work things out on your own?

These are just some of the questions you need to ask yourself. Then, armed with the answers, you can put together a plan that enables you to erect a room for your dreams to become a reality.

Hopes

Hopes can be a bit like dreams. However, they may be more like a 'want' or a 'need'. It can be difficult to define a 'hope'. My dictionary says, 'to wish for or look forward to what one anticipates or expects'. For example, I hope my friend will come to dinner; I hope that I don't get a 'cold' from the person on the bus; I hope that the rain will stop; I hope I can see the kingfisher near the lake, and so on. Hopes are very important. When we are without hope, we talk about being 'hopeless'. There are times when we are without hope. There are times when the situation seems 'hopeless'. I hope for you that these times will be few and far between!

Having a room to hope in is an essential part of our building. I am hopeful that this will be (is) your experience. To create 'hope' one needs to see 'hope'. I think, though, that we all travel through times when all we see is the opposite of 'hope'. For example, we see the problems, the difficulties, the limitations and/or the seeming in-evitable death of our hopes. It is important that these times are only temporary.

Our building has to weather many seasons

I like the analogy of comparing winter to the development of hope. During autumn, death of leaves on trees, grass in fields, and blooming flowers is very evident. In winter, death seems to complete its job. The deciduous trees are bare of leaves; the cold wind and weather takes away the warmth; animals may hibernate and sleep until spring returns. Winter is a time for apparent bareness, bleakness and a lack of life. Actually, this is as far from the truth as the north wind is from the south wind. Did you know that during the long months of winter, resources for new life are developing? Without the sleep of hiber-nation, the hedgehogs would be too exhausted to cope with spring. It would be the same for the trees, the squirrels, and the bulbs beneath the earth. Winter is a time for the regaining of energy. It is the time when hope curls up and takes her nourishment so that, when spring comes, she is ready for new life.

If you feel that you are in a room that is without hope, a room that hides from motivation, a room that seems cold and barren, maybe the hope you need is just asleep? Maybe it needs the warmth of spring to regenerate its awaiting roots? Sometimes hope is rekindled by another, sometimes it's up to us. Are we ready to shake off hope-lessness and plunge into the realms of hope? This can be quite a challenge. You do not have to face this alone, but you can if you wish. Hope is there. When things don't work out the way we expect them to, hope says 'Plan A didn't eventuate, let's explore plan B'.

Achievements

An achievement, a positive outcome from some activity or thought, is also a feeling. It makes us feel good and boosts our morale. We probably have many such occasions every day. However, we don't always notice them. It is an achievement to get up in the morning, get showered, get dressed, get ready for what comes next. It is an achievement to make a decision about something, even a small thing such as what to eat, wear, do or share. There are small achievements and bigger achievements. In our room for achievements we probably need to have both kinds. The important thing is that you notice your achievements even if other people do not!

I quite like listing my achievements. It helps me to get a perspective on my ability rather than always getting stuck on my disability. In fact, it helps me see my different abilities and recognise them too. It's very easy for us to see what we are not good at sometimes. It's even easier for other people to see what we are not good at. At times we endure a lot of negative criticism. This is not constructive and can destroy our dreams and hopes. The best thing to do with it is to pour the weed killer over it! Now negative criticism is different to constructive comment. The latter can be very good for us and very helpful. Constructive comment can help us achieve our goals and should be welcomed. Constructive comment has a place in the room of achievement. An example of negative criticism might be: 'You got a 'C' for your assignment, pity you didn't get a 'B'. Perhaps you will if you try harder next time. An example of constructive comment might be: You got a 'C' for your assignment. Well done, that's higher than a 'D'. Who knows, if you keep this up you might even get a 'B' next time'.

Erecting rooms in our building needs to be planned for. We also need to understand that our needs can change over time and it's OK to adapt to this. Plans can change; we can change with them. If we are not comfortable exploring this on our own then we can share our ideas with a good friend. It is important to stay on task and not take off down side streets that lead us into some dead end alley. Looking at how our lives are shaping and deciding where we want to be and who we want to be may have some bearing upon the types of rooms we erect. Whatever we choose, all of our rooms need to be safe places where we can be free to explore and discover.

What is Love?

I have tulips on the table, bright red buds of life.
When I look at them my smile grows,
I ponder the spring-time and all that it shows;
The new life of ducklings, saplings and bulbs.
This must be love.

I have dinner dished in front of me,
A tasty meal to nourish.
This food enriches my body,
My soul will also flourish.
This must be love.

I encounter some pleasant talking,
I enjoy the woods a–walking,
I feel the sun's face and touch some tender place.
My hurts are all healed as I upward yield.
This must be love.

But what of harsh words and looks that could kill?
Can love reign here too, or is it just still?
Maybe it moves over as pain moves back in,
Maybe it dies when it knows it can't win?
This must be love

Rooms of Pain

I have been to places in my life that I do not wish to return to. In these places there has been much pain and it's very hard to even think of these rooms without feeling that pain. If you have similar experiences you know what I mean. I think that it is important to know that these rooms exist and to be able to visit them, leaving the pain behind. Recently I have been trying to do this. It isn't easy and my first response is to stay well away from such places and leave them alone. The only problem with this, though, is that all the time I choose to do that the pain can still hurt me. I think we have to find a way to visit these rooms, if we need to, but be able to leave the pain there when we leave.

Having said this I do think that there is a time for keeping away. Perhaps the pain is too much, the wounds are too deep? It wouldn't be helpful to go back to that room; it might only serve to increase the pain. Distance from pain and discomfort can be a necessary space that allows appropriate dialogue with oneself so that good foundations for healing can begin. After an appropriate amount of time (this will be different for different individuals) one can begin to revisit those painful places and put together a map of understanding. This might then lead on to either self-forgiveness, forgiveness of other and/or both. I have found that even when an event wasn't my fault, I have a measure of guilt. Allowing myself to accept my emotions, rather than debate with them, is a good place to move on from. If I accept that I have a role to play in any interaction, then I can forgive myself for not being perfect. This way I find that guilt has no sway over me. I believe there are instances of 'false guilt' – guilty feelings which are not based upon reality at all. However, these emotions feel the same as the real thing. Because of this I deal with them in the same way.

Once forgiveness has occurred (this might not make the feelings or the pain go away), I feel free to move on. In my experience when I do this, I close the door on that room. That chapter in my life cannot hurt me any more. I know it happened, I know it's there, but it does not have power over me any more!

When I get stuck

I have noticed that, at times, I seem to go round and round in circles. It's as if I get stuck in an emotion or event that won't let me get off! With relationships, for example, I come to a particular project or person, can get quite obsessive about it, or go to the other extreme and take that person for granted. Either of these responses causes pain because of their extreme and intense apparent reactions from others. I'm still learning, still finding my way around relationships, and negotiating interaction can be a difficult process. Sometimes it is tempting not to bother. Sometimes I just want to close off from everyone and become a hermit…relating to others can seem just too hard! Well, I think we can all benefit from being honest and telling it like it is. Relating is hard for us. This doesn't mean we have to give up, but it might mean that we need help to get it right. If we want to help things work more smoothly, we need to recognise what is happening, why and when. Then we need to work out what to do with it. This whole process can be exhausting and takes up heaps of energy.

I value the support of others and trust my good friend to help me see the way ahead. There is an expression: 'I can't see the wood for the trees'. This means that life can be so full and cluttered that it is blinding me to the reality of the things that really matter. I often ask myself the question: 'Is it urgent? Or, is it important?' Sometimes there exists an urgency that pushes me emotionally, but actually it is not important and I need to get my priorities right, otherwise I will become overloaded very quickly.

Do you remember reading about neurotypical individuals and their being able to divide their attention (**p.19–20**)? Well, this is one reason why they don't seem to become obsessive and can juggle lots of things at once. You and I have all of our attention in one place. This makes it very difficult to 'notice' all the bits and pieces involved in relating to others. We seem to see things as being 'black and white', all or nothing. Learning to recognise that life and relating isn't 'black and white', that it is actually 'grey' at times, can be part of the answer to gaining access to others and moving on. I know this won't be easy, but I do think it is within reach for lots of us.

Checking the plans

When it comes to looking at our building, the rooms we are erecting and the plans that we want to follow, we will need to check in often and match up our plans, hopes, dreams and outcomes with the plan we have. Sometimes, because we are so involved with our building we can get caught out. We might not realise that the room dimensions don't match the plans and we are aiming too high or we have not enough materials and so on. I like to keep my lists of necessary items (hopes, needs, wants, achievements and dreams) close by, so I can revisit them often and see if my plans are working out. If they are not, then I have a chance to check out why and what I might do about it.

Life's project is often a difficult one with so little to assist us on our way. This is one reason why it is so important to have your building safely and firmly erected. Being sure of one place that you can venture out from and return safely into again makes life encounters more tolerable. Some adventures can be wonderful and thrilling. They can be all we hope for and expect. Yet, even these times that give us life, also take life. I can remember not understanding why I felt so 'worn out' when I had had such a great day. Now I understand that even wonderful occasions require my focus and attention.

Giving out of myself in order to enjoy life can use up so much concentration and energy. It can take all that I have just to be there

Reality check

sometimes. Family members have commented 'Why are you so cranky? You were so high a few moments ago'. Yes I was, but now I need space to recoup that lost, expired energy. For many neurotypical individuals, lively, exhilarating encounters feed their energy supplies.

Even though they are tired, they feel renewed and invigorated. So, it might be difficult for them to understand that the things that give us both joy and life, also take life from us. The best thing here is to tell them that yes, you enjoyed the experience but now you need some space to regain your energy.

Key Points

- Our building needs insulation (protection) against the knocks of life and any bad weather.

- When sorting out priorities (needs, wants, rooms) we may need support to help us decide.

- Making dreams a reality can be part of our plans. We can explore this.

- Checking in with our plans to help us stay on track is very useful.

- What rooms do we feel comfortable in?

- Do we have rooms for different events and occasions (hopes, dreams achievements)?

CHAPTER 4

Covering the walls

Presentation of self

This chapter explores the ways in which individuals present them-selves to each other. Presentation of self seems to be a critical issue for polytropic individuals. By this I mean they are particularly concerned with how other people perceive them. This includes their dress, physical appearance and appropriateness in social situations. It is so important to most people that it governs their everyday activities. For example, an office worker before going to work would choose clothes which they see as suitable to their occupation, or a teenager before going to meet his or her friends would put on clothes which they consider cool. In the same way, conversational manner is also chosen, albeit subconsciously, to fit the relationship. For example, teenagers might talk one way to their parents and another way to friends.

For you and me as individuals with autism/Asperger's Syndrome, this presentation of self (wall coverings) might seem awkward, uncomfortable, superficial and unnatural. For example, I have been told that for me to be seen as a credible professional, I have to look the part. Therefore, when I am presenting at a conference I wear my 'presenting clothes'. For me, however, because I'm presenting isn't the only reason I wear these. I also wear them because then I don't have to worry about choosing which clothes to wear! For example, I have 'Saturday clothes', 'Sunday clothes', 'going to visit relatives clothes', 'gardening clothes' 'presenting clothes' and so on. So for me, wearing my 'presenting clothes' is not so much an issue of being appropriate as it is one of lessening the confusion of having to make a choice. However, I am aware that choosing to look like a professional (as far as I can) in professional situations will impact positively upon my credibility. These are important issues, and trying to find a balance whereby one presents appropriately but is still true to oneself is what it's all about.

My father used to say 'clothes maketh the man'. This metaphor means that outward appearance conveys the essence of who we are on the inside. Therefore a person with clean fingernails who is well groomed, well dressed, and speaks well presents the impression that they are well organised, well educated, and can be relied upon. However, appearances can be misleading. Bearing this in mind, one needs always to look beyond appearances, whilst still realising the need to 'cover the walls'.

Noticing the signals

Wall coverings are connected to emotions: they are how emotions are displayed. This means that each and every emotion has its own array of verbal and non-verbal language. I think it is easy for us as individuals with ASD to miss the signals people give out concerning their emotions, unless they are very strong ones. Since strong cues are most often true of negative emotions, so only anger and hostility may be recognised. You might have noticed when a person is cross with you their eyebrows are raised, their voice is raised (is louder than usual), they may raise their hands and so on. These actions accompany their emotive state and are there to demonstrate to you how they are feeling. It all gets rather difficult to understand, however, when we don't pick up on the signals given out to us. We may misinterpret the person's words, actions or both. I can remember when someone pointed at something and all I saw was the pointing finger, not the object that they were pointing at! Because we are not into wall coverings (presentation of self) we may miss the significance of non-verbal actions.

During any conversation, individuals use verbal and non-verbal body language. How to notice what is being said non-verbally can help us understand the context of the conversation. For example, if you meet somebody down the street and they say 'Hello, how are you?', how do you know whether this comment is a form of greeting or whether they really have the time to talk about how you feel? Noting a person's body posture might help to give us some clues. For instance, try to notice whether they are stopped and are faced into you as they speak. If they are, this might mean they have time for a few minutes' conversation. If this is the case, you can respond and also ask how they are. If, however, they are not facing you but keep moving as they talk, you can read their lack of being still as a signal that they don't have the time for more than a few words in passing.

How are you?

Conversation signals

Signals of what a person might be prepared to talk about in a conversation or listen to, could include:

- They show interest in what you are saying by using words like 'tell me more', 'Oh, really?', 'Oh, that sounds good', 'I've noticed that too!' and other words that convey they're happy for conversation to continue.

- Their body posture is usually towards you and they seem focussed on you, as opposed to gazing elsewhere. They tend not to fidget with their bags, fingers, pockets or clothing. They move their arms and head as gestures of interest; usually the gesture goes with the verbal comment; e.g. 'Oh, really?' is said as their head moves to one side slightly. If you're unsure, it's OK to check in with the person and ask them if they have a few minutes to chat or not. If they say they only have a few minutes, this might mean two or three. Be sure to keep your conversation brief. Otherwise people are not keen to converse with us in the future.

If a person is not interested, then they may display the following:

- Verbally, they may use words to signal their lack of interest or lack of time, such as 'I'm in a hurry', 'Can't stop now', 'We must catch up', 'Talk to you later'.

- Non-verbally, their bodies may be in motion, moving away from you as they speak; this signals 'I don't have time to stop and talk'. They may fidget and be restless, sometimes moving their eyes to look at other things, or checking their watch. If you're unsure of their intentions or their needs, it's a good idea to ask if they have the time to chat or need to be getting on with other things.

Interests

Because you and I tend to have deep interests, it might be hard for others to share our appreciations, and vice versa. This can be limiting in conversations for all of us. We want to talk about what we're interested in, but it might not be a mutual interest, therefore it's usually a good idea to check in with the other person to see if they want to talk about the same thing as you. I have said to my son, 'I know it's important for you to talk to me about cars, and I want to listen, however ten minutes talking about cars is good for me and I would like you to listen to me talk about birds for just a few minutes. Is this OK with you?' This way, we both get to talk about things we are interested in. I learn more about cars and Tim learns a little more about Australian birds. There are times when I am not interested in talking about cars or listening to Tim, just as there are times when Tim is not interested in talking about birds. We both agree that it's OK not to talk to each other but to do our separate things.

Body Language

Learning to read the non-verbal signals that people give to each other can take a bit of practice. Neurotypical individuals use facial expressions and body language to punctuate what they say. For example, verbal expressions tend to carry more meaning when they are accompanied by other actions. People often speak to one another with their bodies, as well as with their voices. At times they may be speaking non-literally, but be using literal wording. This can make things very confusing for us. For example, when someone says 'No...you never did!', they actually mean 'Oh wow, you did that?' This kind of animation makes for meaningful conversation between typical individuals. They use lots of hand movements, eyebrow movements, head and whole body movements to add 'meaning' to what is said. This is one of the reasons why you and I can find their conversations so difficult. We tend to say only what we mean. We only use metaphor that makes sense to us and our words are usually literal and precise. I am not so good at reading the unspoken language of people's bodies...but I know it would be helpful to me if I could make more sense of it.

Don't be cross with yourself if you can't learn it all straight away. You may even find that you need time just to study the non-verbal body language of others. This way you can take notes about what people do, where, when and how, and even practise some of these yourself.

I've called this 'wall coverings' because I view body language interaction as superfluous, as 'extra' to the spoken word. However, it does seem rather important to some people, so I thought that understanding it more might be useful. Have you seen how sometimes someone will use words to imply something and then do the opposite? 'No, I shouldn't have any more', as they help themselves to more. 'Yes, I'm fine', as they cry into their handkerchief. 'No, I'm not cross', as they slam the door and walk away. Why do people do this kind of thing? Why don't they like it when we say exactly what we mean, however inappropriate our timing might be?

What are you saying to me?

Theatrics

OK, here goes... I have a theory about this. For neurotypical individuals, I reckon first that it's to do with wanting others to accept and like them. Also, second, I think it's difficult for neurotypical individuals to own some of their feelings. For example, typical individuals can be good at performing (acting) to cover up what they really feel. I think they do this for the reasons I have said. They want to be esteemed as OK individuals who are in control of their lives, and don't really want others to think that they might need someone else to assist them. Western society has set value upon 'not needing others'. It calls this independence. So, rather than show you are in need (weakness), you show you are not (by acting as if you were strong), which is perceived by the individual as 'strength'.

This 'covering the walls' stuff can actually be experienced as a good thing. We might view it as being dishonest and feel rather uncomfortable with the whole idea. I think that with typical individuals, when they feel safe and comfortable, they tend to let their guard down and reveal who they really are and what they really feel. Sometimes they do this only after acting the opposite to how they truly feel. This can be quite confusing, I know. Maybe it's helpful to understand it as a protective shield for them. They need it. Just like you and I might need space and quietness, typical individuals might need social interaction, pretence and even an audience. At times they seem to need permission to be who they are.

A typical person with their defence 'shield' to protect them against being seen as weak

I have found it quite useful to watch, from a safe distance, the antics of others. I learnt a lot about people by observation. Watching television and videos can be helpful too. It's fascinating to observe the way individuals relate to one another. It's like working out a code, deciphering the meanings and then trying to apply them. I think that typical individuals learn how to do this much faster than we do.

Words without pictures

Everyday life is full of everyday activities. We wake up, we get up, we go about our day, which is full of different activities and, sometimes, different people with different moods. Some people seem happy, others do not. At times it can be difficult to tell them apart. In understanding how other people feel I depend a lot upon what they say. For example, a friend shared with me one day a sentence that could be taken several ways. Reading it in print it looked like this: 'Did you sleep in your bed last night?' This seems like a straightforward question (straightforward, on this occasion, means a question without any deviations to it). To help you see different ways of understanding this question I will type the word in **bold** print in each sentence to show where the emphasis might be.

- ○ '**Did** you sleep in your bed last night?' Asks if you **did or did not**?

- ○ 'Did **you** sleep in your bed last night?' Asks did **you**, or did **someone else**?

- ○ 'Did you **sleep** in your bed last night?' Asks did you **sleep**, or **do something else**?

- ○ 'Did you sleep in **your** bed last night?' Asks if you slept in **your bed** or did you sleep in **someone else's**?

- ○ 'Did you sleep in your **bed** last night?' Asks if you slept in your **bed**, or **somewhere else**?

- ○ 'Did you sleep in your bed **last** night?' Asks if you slept **last night** in your bed?

This is a demonstration of how meaning might change according to emphasis. At times, for you and me, meaning can be difficult to decipher. Again, due to our attention being all in one place, we might miss the context of much conversation. When we read, the context is often explained by preceding sentences and those that come afterwards. It can be, therefore, easier to understand 'context' in our reading because of this. However, even in our reading we might miss 'meaning' because we can be so focussed upon the words that we miss 'content'.

When it comes to conversations with others, context can be very difficult to work out. When I'm listening to someone speak, I am focussed upon their talking. I am not looking at their facial expressions or noting their body language. For example, a person might say ' **Oh**, there you are', or they might say 'Oh, **there** you are'. The first sentence emphasises the 'Oh' and shows possible disappointment. The second sentence emphasises the 'there' and says 'at last I found you', suggesting relief. For you and me these differences in tone, intonation and so on can be hard to detect. Neurotypical people tend not to have this difficulty. This might mean they don't realise that we do. It can be very difficult to plan for these types of difficulties. I try to check for my understanding of a conversation by restating what I hear, for example, 'So, what you are saying is…' If I am wrong I am giving the person time to say again, perhaps more clearly, what they mean.

Remember that neurotypical individuals are governed by 'social priorities', which we find difficult because social interaction might not be a priority for us.

Wall coverings, both verbal and non-verbal, seem to be so important to most people and most people use them. But we need to know how to use them appropriately. The faithful presentation of emotion may be possible with people we trust. However, I still check in with my good friends just to be sure that it is OK to sincerely express my feelings without any disguise or concealment. In some situations we may need to monitor what we reveal to others, where, when and how; in other situations, which are safe and/or necessary, we can share exactly how we feel. I am suggesting that we need to be more adaptable. Below I outline some general 'wall coverings' or emotions that you may find helpful to disguise or conceal.

Physical pain, for some of us, can go unnoticed for long periods of time. We often have a high pain threshold and, as long as our attention is elsewhere focussed, we may miss the pain signals. I know that for me, when I notice that I have physical pain, I then find it very difficult not to focus upon it. You may have noted that some neurotypical individuals may feel the need to disguise their physical pain. By disguising I mean that they 'put on a brave face' and don't constantly go on and on about their pain. I believe that they do this because some individuals are upset by the 'moaning and complaints' of others. Therefore, part of caring for them is to refrain from complaining. However, to be true to yourself and to care for you, it might be important to share any physical pain that you have with a good friend. You could even ask for their advice if you think you may need to see a professional about your pain. Pain is very debilitating and there is a lot that can be done to help us cope with pain, especially if it's the kind of pain that is long term.

Emotional pain can really make people around us feel uncomfortable. I'm not sure why this is so. Perhaps it is because emotional pain is often a common experience and many people can identify with it. I usually try to share this type of pain only with friends that I know well and trust. I might mention it briefly to someone else, if asked if I am OK. It's OK to mention you feel miserable, hurt or depressed, but I try to only say it once and only if I am asked about how I feel. Unfortunately, quite often when someone asks how we are feeling, they don't really want you to answer them, unless they are a very close friend. It's just one way of saying 'Hello'. The best answer is a short answer of 'Oh, I'm fine, how are you'? If the person who asks you the question then goes on to answer your question in some detail, it's OK to let them talk for as long as they choose to, providing you have the time to listen.

Dislike of others is something one might feel, but shouldn't generally express. If you are like me you might find this one difficult. However, learning to keep your feelings to yourself might save you from getting into trouble. It's OK to dislike someone, but it's not usually OK to show or tell them you dislike them. If someone you dislike is causing you real discomfort, aim to be polite but limit your interaction with them.

Undivided attention can really occupy a lot of time. I tend to be obsessively interested in the things that interest me and find it difficult when not everyone else is interested in the same things. In fact, they may not be interested at all and don't want me to talk about these things. Or they may 'pretend' to be interested just to be polite. I'm not sure why it's OK to pretend to be interested, when you are not, but it seems to be connected with not wanting to upset another person. To get around this one, I sometimes say that I can stay and chat for only a short time, say half an hour. This way I don't upset them when I need to leave and they won't be cross when I go.

Jealousy can be a nasty feeling for the person who owns it and for the person who is on the receiving end. It tends to occur when an individual wants what they don't have but sees someone else having. This can apply to material gain (money, job, career), relational gain (partner, baby, outgoing personality), educational gain (education, school, status) and other areas of 'gain' (independence, health, friends). Sometimes jealousy will disguise itself by being nice, friendly and seemingly kind. Then it will attack you by saying horrible things about you to others, or by being in a mood with you, so that you feel bad. It might lead a person into doing and saying very destructive things and is not a good emotion.

Revenge is another nasty feeling and very uncomfortable for all concerned. I think that the individual who takes revenge out on another does so for two reasons. First, they are very hurt and very angry and they want the person they feel hurt by to suffer, as they are suffering. Second, I think that they hope it might make the person that hurt them realise that what they did was wrong and they should pay for it. The vengeful action is the payment, or the 'just reward'. However, I don't think revenge has this effect upon its intended victim. Rather, I think it may cause the victim to feel injustice and even trigger revenge in them. So, the cycle just keeps repeating itself and pain continues for all.

Anger, unlike revenge, can be justified. Sometimes we have a right to feel anger and yet we may try to disguise it. We may feel that it is inappropriate to express our anger, so we 'bottle' it up. Some say that depression is introverted anger, or anger going on deep inside us that we can't deal with. Explosive anger might get us into trouble, but disguising it and keeping it buried inside us is also not good. We can even get sick if we do this. Anger management can be quite difficult and sometimes we need support in discovering how to manage our anger. If you think you might need support or guidance in dealing with anger, you could check this out with your local community centre or professional clinician, who could direct you to the appropriate service.

Love is a tricky emotion. We can feel love in various ways, intensity and in a number of situations. I once heard that there were three different kinds of love; love for self, love for family, and romantic love (for your partner). I also heard that family love and romantic love can only occur if we have self love first, as a foundation to all other loves. A good friend once told me that you can only feel romantic love for one person at any one time. If you attempt to 'love' two people at once, then you will eventually come to resent one and prefer the other. She said 'Your heart cannot be in two places at once'. I'm not sure that I agree with her sentiment. However, I do see the conflict and pain this can cause, and the extent individuals go to, to cover up the fact that they maybe loving more than one person at one time, is quite extreme. It also seems to be a very common situation. Disguising one's emotions in this area and not being honest about them is one way that individuals 'cover the walls' and 'cover their tracks'.

Women with Asperger's Syndrome

This book does not, in general, distinguish between the genders of various individuals with Asperger's Syndrome. We are all different, whatever our gender. However, I do think that at times women are the ones who are expected to bring 'the closeness' into a relationship. Traditionally men have been accepted as being less emotional, less domestic and less 'needy' in these areas. Men who may be committed to their work and not so socially connected are not seen as odd so much as they are seen as being 'men'! Women who display the same qualities, however, may be viewed as being odd. Our 'oddness' appears to stand out more because we may not fit traditional roles and rules. I mention this for your information really. What you do with it, if anything, is up to you. I will also add that, at times, women amongst women have quite specific but unspoken rules about 'women's talk'. If you are a woman and find yourself in a predominantly women's group socially, you may be expected to talk about fashion, clothes, make-up, hair, children, partners and home decoration. You might find that others will not understand you if you don't stay with these rules about women's talk!

Autism: My Gender

My gender and I are a package.
We come as part of the deal.
'But autism shows far more damage'.
'Look at the things that you feel'.

I cannot account for these feelings.
Emotions intense and extreme.
But my issues with everyday dealings,
Can cause me to rant, shout and scream.

I don't desire the 'make-up'.
Fashion and high-heels don't appeal.
I don't like perfume or my hair cut,
But my need for 'understanding', is real.

The expectations placed upon me,
Being female and all,
Push me further into pain and grief,
With my back against the wall.

'I cannot multi-task', I say.
'But you must, You're a woman. You can'.
You must cook, clean, organise and play
The role that supports your man.

Your children and men depend on you,
You must be strong, in control and sure.

'What if these things I cannot do?'
'What if my timing is poor?'

'You must work harder, try harder to be,
What society says and dictates'.
'But both my autism and gender are me, you see'
They both influence my states'.

As a woman I function differently.
As a woman I think, see and feel.
As a woman I value all that is me.
My autism is part of the deal.

Key Points

- 'Wall coverings' represent emotions and the way people present to others.

- Emotions can feel very intense.

- Some emotions need to be expressed but others can pass by without expression.

- There are two types of pain, physical pain and emotional pain, but they may feel similar. Knowing how to recognise them and when to tell someone about them is important.

- Revenge and anger may feel similar in our experience but revenge is never OK.

- One needs to know love in order to be able to love oneself and then be free to love another.

- Being a female with ASD might be different and mean different things than it does if you are a male with ASD.

CHAPTER 5

Plumbing and electricity

Energy and waste systems in my building

Plumbing and electricity provide vital connections for any real building. Within the context of this book, they will refer to various systems that carry both good and positive interactions as well as taking away the waste products that are not needed any more. For example, in a real building the plumbing brings water into the home for washing yourself, drinking, washing clothes, washing dishes and flushing the toilet. In our building, which is ourselves, the systems will refer to all activities that connect us to the outside world, carrying in good things necessary to life and taking away our waste.

Electricity provides the energy source that gives power to many of the things needed in a building. In the building of our lives we also need energy and power.

Thoughts

Sometimes a thought springs to mind that will then lead us to action. When I use the term 'springs to mind' I see a water fountain or spurt of water carrying my ideas. My friend, however, sees an idea that bounces up into her consciousness as if propelled by a metal spring, or from a trampoline. These are two different images for the same metaphor. However, the implications are the same. Things come to mind that we can either use constructively, non-constructively, or disregard. These may be in the form of words, ideas, hopes, dreams, signs, notions, attitudes or images. Juggling these thoughts, seeing where they fit or belong, can be difficult. They can provide us with power to accomplish things or they may take away our life. Learning how to channel thoughts and words into the appropriate system takes time and effort!

Having talked about words previously, exploring their potential impact upon us, I won't go into great detail again here. However, just to echo what was said before, words have the power to build our lives or destroy them, so understanding this concept is very important. Learning to use self-talk that builds confidence and restores faith in ourselves is part of nourishing our lives. Devising a system that is part of our routine can be helpful here. I routinely challenge my thinking when I encounter negative emotion, such as anxiety, guilt, and/or fear, to try to put the emotion into the appropriate perspective. At times I need to share my thoughts and feelings with a good friend. This helps me understand my thoughts and feelings more clearly, leading to appropriate action, if any. Another person's viewpoint also helps to illuminate the situation, helping me to sort and organise my thoughts and feelings. I sometimes find it difficult to know which feeling I'm supposed to have when, where and how!

Let's separate our systems into two categories, internal and external, and then explore the tributaries from both.

Internal systems

I have heard it said that we are what we think, and that we are what we eat. These metaphors mean (1) the thoughts we have are linked to the emotions we feel, which then govern our actions, and (2) if we eat rubbish, we feel like rubbish. If we eat a healthy, balanced diet, we tend to feel healthier and more balanced. Feeling balanced might mean spending appropriate amounts of time and thought on various activities, not experiencing dramatic mood swings, engaging in healthy relationships, and feeling a sense of order within ourselves. This can be a difficult process for us as people with Asperger's Syndrome, with our monotropic disposition.

We are what we think and what we eat

Thoughts often consume a large amount of time and may be prone to being obsessive. I sometimes write my thoughts down and then order them into categories; for example, thoughts about what I should or shouldn't do, about when I should or shouldn't do things, what and who I should include (work, family, leisure, diet, sleep, reading, etc.) Then I decide which need to be acted on and how I should act on them, and which can be ignored or discarded. Sometimes sorting out which thoughts are important and which are there to waste my time is very difficult. When I find occasionally I can't do this, again I share my thoughts with my good friend who helps me decide what to do.

Attitudes

Attitudes are often formed inadvertently and over time. Attitudes affect our everyday thinking, processing, concerns and interactions with others. Some of our attitudes are healthy; others, although benign, may actually be doing us harm. For example: critical attitudes towards oneself and/or others may alienate both self and others. These types of attitude need to be conveyed to the waste system.

I think that many of us with Asperger's Syndrome or monotropic dispositions are inclined towards perfectionism. We often only see one way of having, doing or saying something, therefore when an event, outcome or interaction doesn't match our expectations, we reject it. For example, if I think that dinner should be at six thirty, but it isn't ready until six thirty five, I can feel misled, not cared for; dinner *has* to be at six thirty, and so on. My thinking is locked into one theme, one conception, one perception and I find it very difficult to see and accept other viewpoints or to have an extended viewpoint.

Useful approaches

What I think might be helpful here are the following:

○ Writing a list of possibilities and alternatives beyond the one that you think is appropriate. For example, dinner is usually at six thirty but sometimes it's OK if it's a bit later or earlier. We usually have dinner at home but it's OK to have dinner outside of home, in a café, somebody else's home or in the form of a picnic. Dinner is allowed to take various forms, occur at differing times, have a different name (tea, supper), and be eaten in different places.

○ Checking with a good friend their view or perspective on the situation, and considering their view may be valid and relevant. Sometimes their viewpoint may be more accurate or appropriate or relevant than mine and this is OK. We can even choose to let go of our belief. If we find that both our viewpoint and that of our friend are of equal value, maybe we can accept them both. At times, we will not like another person's viewpoint and may not agree, and that's fine too.

○ If we feel that we are upset or disturbed when our expectations are not met, we can explore this feeling and our attitude towards it. This might mean talking to our good friend or writing some things down to help gain access to the full picture of what's going on inside us. It's OK to feel disturbed (it might not be nice or comfortable) but usually we can resolve it by working through the processes outlined above.

○ Developing helpful attitudes towards ourselves and others is a process that takes time and energy. Firstly we need to understand that a particular attitude would be helpful. For example, learning to accept myself even with the things I don't like about myself, and even accepting others in the same way. Sometimes it is very difficult to see which attitudes are helpful and which are not, therefore again it is good to check this out with a good friend.

External systems

Diet

External systems, or interactions outside of who we are, will directly or indirectly influence who we are. For example, eating a healthy diet and gaining the right nourishment for our physical body will also influence our emotions and wellbeing. Sometimes for individuals with Asperger's Syndrome, foods that are high in wheat, gluten and dairy products can cause problems. The sort of problems some people experience are increased mucus, hyperactivity, skin irritations, lowered resistance to infection, and bowel problems. If you believe this could be happening for you, it's good to check it out with your general practitioner or a nutritionist. It's also important to be sure that you are having sufficient minerals and vitamins in your diet. Some of us have found the B group of vitamins and vitamin C particularly helpful.

Exercise

Exercise is an essential everyday part of feeling good about who we are. I am not very good at being around lots of people, so sometimes I choose to walk at times of the day when it's less busy. I have even been known to sit on my exercise bike and pedal whilst watching the television or a video. Whether it's walking the dog, walking to the shop, walking up and down steps and stairs, or even walking the length of your room several times, exercise does you good. Choosing to exercise outdoors whenever possible is a good option, but if it's not available to you, take the indoor one.

Even though team sports might not be your forte, you could consider individual sports such as cycling, walking, running, roller blading or swimming. If you want to join a team, however, explore your options. You might like to consider a team sport with very clear rules and boundaries, such as lawn bowls or ten-pin bowling.

Agencies

Although your best agency is yourself, you can explore agents outside of you that specialise in particular provisions. For example, youth groups, chess clubs, cycling clubs, computer clubs, walking groups, scrabble clubs and so on. You also might find the internet a useful resource. There are specific agencies and support groups on the internet for individuals with Asperger's Syndrome, as well as particular forums for specific interests.

The other types of agencies which might be helpful in fuelling both internal and external systems are the community resources funded by local governments. It is important when considering one's plumbing needs, to explore available options. This can be done as we take in words, thoughts, attitudes and any other life-giving resource. We also need a system for taking away the waste and/or unnecessary products. I find keeping a journal recording my thoughts, ideas and experiences, a useful tool in helping me decide what should be coming into my life and what I should be getting rid of. I also find that I do need someone to talk to and explore these options with.

Plumbing needs

Power (electricity or gas)

For me the most energising and empowering source that gives me life tends to come from two main areas; interest and relationships. This might be different for you. You may like to think about where you get most of your 'life' from. For some individuals it might be the computer, for others it might be a particular project. It really is important to identify the things that feed you and give you energy. It is important to recognise your personality disposition. For example, if you are a shy, quiet, introverted person, you are more likely to gain life and energy from solitary pursuits, whereas if you are an outgoing, extroverted person, you are more likely to gain life and energy from spending time with other people (interaction may be by the internet, phone or in person). At times I know that my interests have a particular, obsessive component to them. I accept that this is how it is for me and I try to ensure that my obsession doesn't rob me of life. I do this by setting boundaries for myself. For example, I only allow myself a certain amount of time on my computer and then I take time away from it. I might go for a walk, watch some television, telephone a friend, bake a cake and so on. This is important to do, because otherwise the very thing that gives me life might be the thing that burns my life and overloads me.

Choosing the best

As any tradesman would know, you need the right tools for the job. It is not wise to use paper glue on wood. It wouldn't be helpful to use a shifting spanner when you need a pair of pliers. Hammering a screw into position might seem a useful solution if you don't have a screwdriver, but it will render the screw useless for any future applications.

Locating the best tool for the job can be compared to tapping into the right power source that gives the most life. Why choose to exist on low energy levels when you could access higher ones? For example, why use candles for light if you want to read, when you could access a more efficient reading light. Candles are great for creating a relaxing atmosphere, and have their uses, but electricity produces a much better light for reading by. Therefore, if you find yourself in a relationship or an obsessive interest that appears to rob you of life, you might need to re-evaluate the place of this relationship or interest in your life. Such situations may be depleting your energies rather than adding to them.

Take the following energy test:

1. Do you feel tired after this event?

2. Are you looking forward to this event?

3. Does this event consume more time than any other event?

4. Can you easily let go of this event?

5. Do you feel replenished after this event?

6. Does this event make you feel good about yourself?

7. Does this event make you feel bad about yourself?

8. Does this event make you feel good about yourself, even though it may make you feel tired?

9. Does this event lead into other opportunities?

10. Does this event have positive outcomes for you, even though the event itself might not have been entirely enjoyable?

If you answered yes to questions 2, 4, 5, 6, 8 , 9 and 10, and no to questions 1, 3 and 7, this event gives you energy. If you had different answers to the above, you may need to revisit this event and query its energy-giving properties.

Connections

I have noticed that for me, feeling connected to life is related to whether I feel the following: interested, at home, comfortable, accepted, in a reciprocal situation, in a meaningful situation, that I have value and that I am able to use my skills and abilities to the maximum possible extent. Although I tend to feel disconnected when the above factors are not in operation, I am maintained by structure. This means that although I often feel disconnected from feelings of life, this does not have to be a barrier to living. Having my daily life structured, organised and made as predictable as possible, gives me life. You might feel the same way, you might not. The important thing, though, is that you know what gives you life, what doesn't and what you can do about it.

Antisocial versus unsociable

Some individuals have said to me 'Get a life'. I believe that there are many valid ways of 'having a life'. For example, staying home, reading books, working by yourself in the garden, chatting on the internet, partying, clubbing, going for long solitary bike rides or walks etc. are all equally valid ways of living your life. Finding that you feel more comfortable in less sociable situations does not make you antisocial. Antisocial behaviour is when an individual's behaviour is destructive, aggressive, undermining, hurtful to others, inconsiderate and/or soul destroying. It does not build the common morale or empower the individual at all. However, being unsociable does not automatically mean that one is any of the above; it just states 'I feel more comfortable in less sociable situations', such as one to one interaction, being by myself and other such choices. These situations and feelings are quite legitimate and empowering for the individual concerned.

Power may come from other sources

Amenities can be likened to the outside agencies that you and I might need to utilise. This covers everything from libraries, community centres, clubs, restaurants, hotels, to government run facilities and operations. You might also need to access agencies such as employment agencies, medical centres, insurance companies, law firms and the like. Making use of all these resources is your right. However, if like me you have problems with people and paperwork, you may need support to access these.

Keeping warm

Protecting oneself against the cold, hostile and inaccessible world around us can be a daunting task. Choosing appropriate support and knowing how to utilise it is quite an art. I have made many blunders in (1) locating appropriate support and (2) maintaining it. First, it's important to get to know yourself: your likes, dislikes, what you cope with or don't cope with, what your comfort zone is and so on. Second, it's important to take your time in getting to know individuals you choose to relate to. Don't be in a hurry to share deep and meaningful aspects of who you are. It's OK to let a relationship unfold slowly; building security within a relationship takes time. Always work within your comfort zone, but aim at getting to know the other person's, too.

At home I have an electric blanket on the bed in the spare room. I can choose when to turn this on and off, how long to leave it on for, and who to put it on for. I can ask a guest who might be sleeping on that bed if they would like the blanket on, and show them how to do it. Accessing the energy in a relationship and knowing how to direct the flow works two ways. However, a relationship is not like an electric blanket. Most relationships need nurturing, monitoring and maintaining. Choosing to relate and be connected to life takes lots of energy, but also gives back at least as much as you put into it, if not more. Interdependence is the ideal; living independently is not the same thing. Learning how to share resources with others is a good thing and may be part of learning how to keep warm in a society that can be cold and unforgiving.

Key Points

- What am I bringing into my life?

- Are there things I need to rid my life of?

- Am I taking care of me?

- Am I eating a balanced diet?

- What would be a good way for me to get my exercise?

- Am I making use of outside agencies (education, support, home-help, counselling)?

- What is the state of my relationship to and for others?

CHAPTER 6

Past influences upon how we build our lives

How we encounter life and how life encounters us may have a lot to do with the settings in our growing years. Did we grow up in the town or in the country? Where were we educated? Was it in rural or urban territory? Where do we get our value system from? Do we have traditional thinking about traditional values, religion, employment, gender, sexuality? What caused us to make up our minds about these things? Are we just as set in our thinking today as we were when we were younger, or has it changed?

During my growing years we moved around a lot. Between the ages of three and four we actually moved three times in the same street! Although in many areas of my life I am a person who does not like change, I do enjoy travelling. Perhaps the basis for this like is set in our constant moving when I was a child. Moving was routine for me. Today when I am at home I last for maybe a month before I get the feeling that I need to get out of these four walls. So a train journey to go visit friends in a not too far away town is perfectly manageable. At times even just to go for a day trip out to a different part of the ocean without interacting with any other people is also perfectly reasonable. I think that the settings we have experienced as children have a lot to do with what we're comfortable with as adults.

You may be an individual who didn't move house a lot as a child, but still enjoy travelling. You may be an individual who did move house a lot as a child, and now you don't like travelling. Whoever you are and whatever your experiences, it is most likely the settings of your childhood are impacting on your adult life in one way or another. We can each experience the same event but encounter it very differently simply because we are different people! Sometimes we cannot even trace from childhood what the impact was, where it came from, or why we do particular things as adults now. Possibly we do not even need to try to. The main thing is to understand that our current attitudes, understandings, values and expectations, in one way or another, probably have their roots in childhood. In other words, we didn't suddenly become who we are today, it's been a process over time.

It might be helpful to write down or list significant points that you remember from your growing years. For example, the houses you've lived in, schools you've gone to, teachers you've been taught by, subjects you were interested in, pets you've had, friendships and interests you've known. The reasoning behind this exercise is to help you locate some of the settings for your current attitudes.

I wondered why I found it difficult to talk about some things. Was it just because I wasn't interested or was there more to the story? For instance, I find it difficult to enjoy some of the interests that other people hold close to their hearts, for example, football. When I think back over the years, my father was a football fan and when football was on the radio and the TV, I was simply an interruption that was not welcome. Consequently, although I don't mind being involved in ball games, I dislike watching or talking about them. So if an individual within my circle of friends is really into football, I find it very difficult to relate to them because this is not one of my interests. In fact, most of my friends would not be football fans and possibly that's been a directive in my choice of friendships.

The reality is that each of us is surrounded by people with many and varied interests, whilst you and I probably only have one or two things that we're passionately interested in. This makes it very difficult to interact with others who perhaps don't share our passion. The danger is that we might therefore close ourselves off from such individuals and choose not to relate to them at all. I say that this is a danger because these people may be within our own families and work situations, and it might appear to them that we are being rude and antisocial. I have found learning to accept that people have different interests to me, but that they are still worthwhile in-dividuals, a very useful understanding. I can choose not to talk to them about their interest, while still listening to them as people. This way I am not seen as rude and impolite, but I don't have to get caught up in conversations that don't interest me.

Skills

We all have skills and abilities that have come from general education and inherent interests. It is a good idea to uncover what we're really good at. You might notice from your lists that particular likes and abilities keep recurring. For example, in my lists I notice that poetry, words, writing, songs, insects, birds and colour keep appearing. My computer is the medium that I use to explore these. It allows me to access words (poetry, songs), information and data about insects and birds, and even other people who relate to these things in the same way that I do. I have always loved words and was never really any good with numbers, so arithmetic and mathematics is very difficult for me. I accept that I need help with issues based around money and the financial business of everyday life. Needing other people in my life is a good thing, not a weakness.

Knowing what our skills are and knowing what we are not so skilled at is an asset. This knowledge can be helpful in our employment and relational situations. If you find yourself in a job which is causing great discomfort, maybe you need to ask yourself why. Does it have something to do with the settings of your growing years? Does it have anything to do with your skills and abilities? Are you perhaps in a situation that you were not designed for? Do you need to consider making some changes? If you think you do need to make some changes, talking about it to a good friend or an agency that explores individual potential might be a good idea.

Doors

When I go to the cinema, I like to sit near the entrance, which at times is also the exit. I need to know where the ladies' toilets are. I also need to know where the kiosk is. I like to be able to get an ice cream during the intermission. You might think, what has this got to do with everyday life? Well, knowing when to enter a conversation and leave it, or enter a group and leave it, have a similar nature. We each need to be able to recognise the entrance sign and the exit sign for social interactions. Have a think about what you consider to be the entry and exit points to a conversation. How do you know when it's your turn to talk? How do you know when a conversation has ended and the person wants to move on? How can you tell if someone is interested in continuing with a conversation?

The Group

There were just seven of us,
Seated all around.
The man with the shortest hair
Started to make a sound.
I was quiet.

I wanted to keep watching,
There were Blue Tits in the tree.
The man said something louder,
'Oh, did you speak to me'
I said?'

There are blue Tits in the tree'
Said I. There was silence in the group.
The man with the shortest hair
Returned to eating his soup.

'There are Blue Tits in the tree',
I stated just once more.
'Wendy, do you want some tea?'
'Do you want me to pour?'
He said.

'There are Blue Tits in the tree'
I only thought this time.
'Why were they not excited?'
'Could they not enjoy this find'?
They all ate soup.

'Wendy, the waiter needs to clear the plates'
The man with the shortest hair spoke.
'Why does this concern me?' I said.
The girl with long hair spoke,
'You need to eat your soup now Wendy,
Hurry up for goodness sakes'!

What had I done?
What did I not get?
The Blue Tits are gone,
I haven't eaten yet.

At university, when there's a break between the lectures and some of
the students go off together for coffee, I sometimes wish I could go
with them. If I wait to be invited, I usually miss the opportunity. If I
tag along, I'm unsure if I'm doing the right thing. Because it's so
difficult to know, I stay behind in the lecture room and drink coffee
from my flask and eat my piece of fruit alone. At times I am happy to
be on my own, but at other times I wish I could join the group. The
following are some possible scenarios that may help in our deciding
how, when and where to join a particular group.

○ Is this group one we would like to be part of?

○ Does this group want us to join them?

○ Is it possible to be part of this group? For example, do we
  live in the same vicinity? Can we get to meetings and so on.

○ Will this group be able to accommodate our interests?

○ Will we be able to accommodate their interests?

You need to find the answers to the above questions before joining
the group. It's not a good idea to just join yourself to a group without
knowing it's OK to be there. You could move towards a group and say
'Is it OK if I join you?' This way, you are giving the group permission
to answer honestly and give you an entry or an exit. At times, a group
will say 'Yes, please join us' or words to this effect, but it does not
mean that they always want you to join them, so you still need to

check in each time. You will also need to be attentive to the group conversation and the group interest. Sometimes the group will be interested in what you have to say; sometimes you need to listen to the group interest. I have also found it useful to check in with the group as to how long I can stay and talk; when the group needs to move on to other things; and when the conversations need to finish. Knowing when to exit from a group situation is just as important as knowing how to enter one. If we suddenly place ourselves into a group without an invitation and then pour out our own interests or agenda, the group will feel very uncomfortable. It might mean the group will not want us to join them again. This is similar to the ways in which one enters and exits conversations.

Belief Systems

I have been very set in my belief systems and felt really convinced that 'my way' was the best way. I even believed, at times, that my way was the only way. I'm not quite so sure of these things now. It is fine to be unsure at times. We can explore our surroundings, revisit our feelings and the items that we have been so set with and double-check them. Even if we come up with the same belief system, it's perfectly OK to let others have a different belief system. Some individuals might appear set against us. If we explain things to them they might change their view of us. However, this is not guaranteed.

I use to think that if I missed out on the order of a 'plan' or things didn't go quite according to my plans, that this was awful and terrible. However, someone explained to me that, for example, feeling 'awful' and 'terrible' are strong emotions that belong to serious situations. For example, when one jumps out of a plane and the parachute fails to open, this is awful and terrible. When plans don't work out according to one's expectation then one feels uncomfortable. This isn't very nice and it can pose quite a dilemma, but it isn't terrible.

Choice and decision-making

There are some fundamental assumptions when it comes to making a choice. It doesn't matter whether it's a choice concerning food, which TV program to watch, whether or not to go for a walk or if you need to put on more clothing. Whatever the choice is about, it assumes that you can decide what you want, what you need and what to do about it. I don't know if this is true for you, but for me, choice is very difficult and I'm not too keen on it! Because of this, I often repeat decisions that I have made in the past. I choose to wear the same clothes; I watch the same TV programs; I walk the same routes and at the same time of day; I say the same words to people; I have a particular way of preparing for bed at night; and I like to eat the same foods.

These set routines can be an issue if I am with people who want different things than I do. Maybe they would choose to watch a different TV program than the one I want to watch. Maybe they will choose to eat a meal other than the one I usually eat! Most of my discomfort about these things comes from not being accustomed to doing something differently, and therefore not knowing how it will be for me. To help myself with this difficulty, I find it useful to attempt to do different things at times. For example, lately I have been attempting to eat some new food combinations. They might not be new to people who are used to eating a wide variety of different things, but they are new to me. To my surprise and joy, I have found, so far, the foods have been very nice. I also tried shopping for some new clothes and found that I liked to do this as well. I only go to the shops at quiet times of day. I only choose similar clothes to those I am happy to wear. I always try the clothes on in the shop's changing room and I only buy two items of new clothing at any one time. I have a budget to help me decide how much money I can spend and I aim to stay within my limits.

The good thing about all of this is that I am the one in control. I can choose what I think I might like, and it's OK if I don't always get it right. I'm sure that there will be some foods that I don't like. I'm sure that I will come across some clothes that I may initially choose to wear and then change my mind. It is perfectly OK to change one's mind about these things. It is also fine to be unsure and a bit nervous about trying something new. The good news is that we can always go back to what's familiar if we need to. The other good news is that we can choose the same things to do, say, think, feel and be, if we need to. The down side of this choice is that it might be a bit limiting for us and we might miss lots of great opportunities for good experiences. But, hey, we are in control, it's up to us.

Processing information

Do you find that sometimes during a conversation you are just beginning to understand what the person is talking about when they decide it's time for them to stop talking? I know I am slower to process information than lots of other people I see talking to one another. Most other individuals I know seem to be able to respond to one another fairly quickly. I need time to process the spoken word. I also find it easier to make sense of a conversation if the person talking to me doesn't stand in front of me and expect eye contact. In fact, if they stand to the side of me I hear them better. I think it is fine to tell the person talking to us that we prefer them to stand wherever it's the most helpful for us. This might vary for different individuals and at different times. The thing is, if we don't let people know, they might not realise the difficulty for us. They might just think we are slow, rude or not interested.

What did you say?

At times I need information written down for me. You might find this helpful too. People tend to talk quite fast and expect us to keep up with them. If I can't, then I let them know. Most people are happy to slow their pace down and give us less information all at once, if we ask them to. Having the information in writing is also helpful. I know this is difficult if it's an ordinary conversation, but if it's information needed for a job or an activity, this should be fine.

Understanding our role

I used to wonder how someone could be 'so many things, to so many people'. It's not hard to understand that I am my mother's daughter, mother to my own children and sister to my siblings. However, all these roles have different expectations attached to them. How does one sort out which action, emotion and character goes with which identity? Do we need to explore this? Maybe this isn't an issue for you. If it isn't, that's OK. I have found that my role expectations can be a bit confusing, though, and I get muddled about which belongs to whom! This has meant that, at times, I have shared personal information which wasn't appropriate and, at other times, I have withheld information that I should have shared.

I think that, if you are neurotypical, you might be inclined towards 'feeling' which words, actions and emotions are right for which people and which situations. However, I and other individuals I know with autism and Asperger's Syndrome might miss the cues and clues to this knowledge. Therefore, it can be quite useful to have some form of a guide or check list to help out. You can write your own guide with your own situations in mind. Below are some general principles that might be helpful:

- Name of the role (eg. friend, client, employee)

- Identity of the role (eg. informal relationship, formal relationship, long term, short term)

- Words and actions typical of this role (eg. personal and shared, informative, helpful and cooperative).

If you write down the information that applies to you and your relationships, you might get a better idea of what's appropriate and what isn't. Sometimes, no matter how hard I try to get it right, I don't succeed. This is not generally irreparable. I may need to apologise and try again, if I'm given the chance.

Key Points

- Our past impacts upon our present. How is this true for you?

- Are you using your skills and interests in the building of your life?

- What doors are open for you? Do you need to open some more? Do you need to close some that are only leading you nowhere?

- What is motivating the building of your life? What do you believe about who you are? What do you believe about others?

- What have you learnt from your decisions? Is your building accommodating of change, difference and plans that were not expected?

- How do you process your plans for understanding yourself and others? Are you a 'feeling' person or do you need a mental picture of your plans?

CHAPTER 7

My building in relationship to my neighbours

The Friendship Song

Some say that Summer will warm a fragile heart.
Others talk of music, or of walking in the park.
But Winter isn't always the reason for the cold,
It maybe icy outside, Spring or Summer bold.
The hurting soul feels nothing, except the pain untold.

Chorus

When words are shared with another,
A secret world unfolds.
The joy of true acceptance
Brings you inside, out from the cold.

You took my hand and travelled too.
Through wind and rain, we sailed, us two.
My hurting heart, so torn apart,
Was wooed to life by you.

Chorus

When words are shared with another,
A secret world unfolds.
The joy of true acceptance
Brings you inside, out from the cold.

My heart is stronger now, and warm,
As we continue upon Life's way,
We wake to face another day.
For, together we will brave the storm

Chorus

When words are shared with another,
A secret world unfolds.
The joy of true acceptance
Brings you inside, out from the cold.

Truer friends the world knows not,
Thank you, my friends to me.
So while the seasons come and go,
The Summer rains or Winter snow.
I wish you only love to know.
For life will pass, but as we go,
Hear the pain of each other's soul.

Chorus

When words are shared with another,
A secret world unfolds.
The joy of true acceptance
Brings you inside, out from the cold.

Building my life will include others

Whatever my family make-up, I will inevitably have to have dealings with others. I may be used to living in a family with parents, brothers, sisters, aunts, uncles and so on. I may be an only child without any extended family members to relate to. I'll need to visit shops, agencies, and other situations where people frequently gather. I may need to travel on a bus or a train, and I won't be able to always predict that I can sit alone, or that the person next to me won't want to talk to me. In various aspects of my everyday life, I will encounter other people, and I'll need to know how to relate, whether to be casual or formal and so on.

At times, I have found it really difficult to know if, when a person is looking at me, it means they want to talk to me or if they just happen to be gazing in my direction. I now know that I don't have to work out or answer that question. I can just allow the person to look without knowing why. I can leave the decision to the other person, and allow them to decide if they wish to talk to me or not. This way, I don't waste time in trying to work out the scenario. Discovering that other people have choices and can make decisions has released me from a lot of responsibility that wasn't mine in the first place. Other people can tell us what they want from us.

When I go to the shop to buy the groceries, it's perfectly OK just to do the shopping and then leave. If I pass another person doing their shopping and they say 'Hi', I'm allowed to say 'Hi' back and leave it at that. If they say 'Hi, how are you doing?', I am allowed to answer 'Fine thank you, how are you?' and leave it at that. If they stay talking and standing still, they may wish for a slightly longer conversation. However, this probably is not the right situation to converse about my (or your) special interest. If you did happen to meet someone who had the same interest as you, and wanted to stand and talk about that interest, this would be fine to do. The important thing is, if you are not sure, you can check it out with the person and give them the opportunity to tell you whether they are free to talk or whether they need to keep going.

Coping with self

Self-acceptance, self-esteem or self-respect can be problematic in autism and Asperger's Syndrome, because the world around us often says that we are odd, strange, difficult, egocentric and social misfits. Who makes the rules for what is odd, strange, egocentric and socially misfitting, however, is debatable. Many individuals who would be considered as neurotypical, successful and socially fluent, may be surrounded by problems with family, work, lovers and other people in general. Yet, they would see themselves as 'normal' and us as not! Sometimes it is our honesty, black and white concepts about right and wrong, and our commitment to these, that separates us from them. I think they find this uncomfortable and even embarrassing. I can respect myself because I am true to who I am. Our self-esteem is built upon the foundation that yes, we are different from the neurotypical population, but we have much that they envy and much that they do not possess. Coping with my difference, with our difference, is built upon the foundation of diffability, not disability. I am only disabled in a neurotypical world where my ability is not recognised or utilised!

Coping with others

Learning to accept and respect myself is one thing but how do I learn to respect others? It is difficult to respect people who enjoy gossip, who seem to talk about nothing important and who may enjoy putting others down (saying they are not as good as them). Respect can be earned, yes, but it can also be attributed to someone or something as a right. I respect the insects that crawl through my garden. They didn't really do anything special to earn my respect, I just give it to them. I think that this is the kind of respect I need to have for all other individuals. My father used to say 'Do unto others as you would have them do unto you'. This is a biblical reference that implies we should 'treat other people the way you want them to treat you'. This is the first step in coping with other people. I only need to ask myself one question: 'Do I want that person to treat me that way?' If my answer is 'Yes', then all well and good. If the answer is 'No', then maybe my behaviour isn't the best.

In coping with others I always expected them to know what my needs were. This isn't really fair, because they probably don't know what I need if I haven't told them.

Difference

Sometimes it's hard to appreciate that not everyone is like us. My life may be highly structured. I may enjoy dwelling in a particular room in my building. I may have set routines and like things done in a particular way. Other people however, may like to be spontaneous, live unstructured lives and value the spur of the moment decisions that are not planned. For me, events that are not planned and appear out of nowhere are very challenging and cause me great anxiety. Difference is OK. I just need to understand that we each do things in a different way.

More plans for daily living

When I was a child, the world went on doing the things it does whether or not I liked them. I didn't feel that I had any control over most of the decisions that affected my life. I wasn't consulted or asked to contribute to these decisions. I think that my parents thought this was best for me. I'm not sure that I agree with their decision to keep me out of the picture, but as an adult, I can understand they thought it in my best interest.

As an adult now, I am mostly in control of my own daily living plan. As I have said, I cannot control other people around me and just as I don't have the right to try to control them, they don't have the right to try to control me. When I was a child, working out what was expected of me was very difficult. It was easier just to attach myself to some 'other' who seemed to understand the world better than I did, and access life through them. This meant that I tended to form 'over attachments' or attachments that didn't allow the other person enough space for themselves. Wendy always needed them! I still have this tendency, but aim to keep it in check. It is helpful that I am more confident in my everyday decisions, and in myself. I can 'trust' myself and I can rely upon what I know. Getting to this place has taken a long time and has been a difficult journey.

Letting go of failure

I think it would have been helpful to me if I'd had some kind of plan to show where I had been and where I needed to go. Maybe we all feel like this, neurotypical and Asperger individuals alike! Planning to see where the building of our life has come to date would be a good place to start. As I think about the plans and how they haven't always worked out, I feel very privileged. Life in the past was often painful, confusing, distressing and difficult. I feel that I let many people down and didn't fulfil their expectations of me. For a very long time I carried guilt about this around with me. Today, however, I realise that such failings are part of what it means to be human. I have a choice in this, I can keep carrying the guilt or I can lay it down, accept that this is all part of learning and take the lessons I have learnt to help equip me for the next part of my life plan.

I have a scripture, which has often comforted me: 'I know the plans I have for you' says the Lord, 'Plans for good and not for evil'. The reason this is comforting is because of the 's' in plans. I once thought that God had a PLAN (only one plan) for my life. When I believed that I had missed this plan, I felt so awful. Now I know that he has several plans! If plan 'A' fails, then I can move to plan 'B'.

Deviation from a plan

A line from a film I once saw said 'We'd all put in for a new past if we could'. This just means that, for most of us, some parts of our life in the past, when we were growing up, when we were teenagers and/or younger adults, were not as satisfying as we would have liked. Maybe we didn't like the decisions others made for us? Maybe we didn't like the decisions we made for ourselves? Maybe we have felt life has been a project that has taken us places we would rather not have gone? Regret might be the feeling that we are left with. You know, when life leads us into plans we were not prepared for and all we see are the problems ahead of us, we cannot always draw upon previous experience to help us out. Sometimes we will find ourselves in new situations that require new plans.

In the past, some of my decisions have not been the best and did not produce the best results. However, they did lead to particular outcomes and I have learnt from these. Although such events might not have been planned for and were not straightforward, I tried to make the most of them. Each of us is faced with building choices in the building of our lives. The difficulty for me, most of the time, however, was that I often wasn't aware that I had a choice, lacked resources to enact any alternatives anyway and simply accepted what was in front of me.

Now, many years later, I try to take more time over the various decisions that confront me. I explore possible outcomes of these by doing some homework. I reach into the experiences of my past and check if I have come across such difficulties before. If I have, where did they leave me, what did they leave me and was I pleased with the course they led me on? If the answer is positive to these questions then I take that into consideration as I explore my plans. If the answer is one that left me wanting it to be different, I explore what other alternatives I might be able to access. If possible, I try to find out where the plan might take me, what might be at the other end waiting for me and what I might encounter if I follow that plan. I often share my concerns with a good friend. My friend might have encountered the same things in the building of their life and may have information about it that could be useful for me in my decision making. Therefore, sharing of mutual experiences could be good for us both.

If all of this exploring still leads me to places that I don't like when I get there, then I tackle it from a different angle. For example, I ask myself the following questions: 'Is this good for me, even though I am uncomfortable with it?', 'Could this experience be useful to me?', 'Might it be that this is the way that I need to go, even though it's unpleasant?' There is a poem that once hung on a wall in my home. The gist of that poem went something like, 'The dark threads are as needful in the weaver's skilful hand, as are those of gold and silver in the pattern he has planned'. You see, you and I may not have access to the completed picture of our lives. We may not know just now, that some of the events in our lives, however dark, will add stature and texture to who we are becoming. I'm not saying that we should simply accept the parts of our building that have been painful, uncomfortable and difficult, as if they were inevitable. No, I'm saying that what we cannot change, because it happened, we can still use for good.

Daily routines

I'm definitely a creature of habit, even though I love to explore. I like to know what the day's plans are and, if I am likely to encounter other individuals during my day, I like to know in advance of this happening. Unfortunately, though, other people may not operate this way and, instead, feel quite comfortable with spontaneity. I'm learning that this is OK for them. Rather than be cross with them for not appreciating where I am coming from, I take the lead and, whilst accepting it might be OK for them, I can let them know kindly that it is not OK for me. I may choose to say something like 'I appreciate your calling over, but this isn't a great time for me. Could we rebook another time (take a rain check)?' This way I hope that they will not be upset, and that we can plan their next visit. With my good friends, I can say freely that I need them to call me before visiting. At times I have accepted visitors who have simply knocked upon my door. They may be neighbours or individuals collecting for a charity. I am still free to choose whether or not to answer the door, whether or not to respond to their requests and in what way I would like to respond. I like the metaphor: 'You cannot stop the bees passing by but you can stop them from nesting in your hair'!

Sometimes because of my need for routine and order, others can misinterpret my actions and consider my needs as egocentric. I actually depend upon knowing what will happen next (my routine) because of my difficulty with predicting of outcomes. Therefore, I am much less stressed when my daily life is pre-planned and organised. If other people don't use tools to help them with their daily living plans, this is fine too. However, if they interrupt mine and expect me to be able just to get back to what I was doing and not feel uncomfortable, their expectation may be too high. We can inform our neighbours (other people in our lives) that this is what we require and ask that they respect this. I too need to learn how to allow others to do things their way, even if it disagrees with the way I like to do things.

As I sit and type these words, it is six o'clock in the morning here in Tweed Heads, New South Wales, very close to the Queensland border in Australia. There is a reddish golden glow appearing in the distance; it is the sun rising. How strange to think that as I am experiencing this new day, others are experiencing the end of their day. You see we all have differing experiences – not just of different events though, even of the same events. Learning to accept this has saved me from lots of potential problems with various encounters with my neighbours. Learning to accept myself and the way I like things; learning to accept that others may have different likes, opinions and thoughts, is all part of the process of building my own life and learning from the personal journey we are each on.

The journey of life

Here in my watery existence life seems calm, muffled and
buffered.
I like it here.
What is this? I'm being pushed! I'm being forced; I'm being
suffered.
I don't like this!
Rough, cold and separated. My life cord is cut.
Home, warm and welcoming, all her doors are shut.

This air I breathe feels jagged and strange,
My throat is dry and raw.
But I remember the watery sounds when Life was arranged,
When all around me was all that I saw.
I liked it then.

This strange and forbidding place begs me stay awhile.
There, surrounding me the voices offer a smile.
At first I push away from them, too strange and scary for me.
Then I accept, unwillingly, that they will help me see.

Learning to trust and feel safe again, what a journey is this.
Up hill and down dale, along busy roads, in clear air and
mists.
Sometimes the road is clearly marked. I know where it will
lead.
At other times though, the darkness stays and yet I must
proceed.
I don't like this.

I want all to be predictable again, just as it all once was.
I may have to accept that this cannot be,
I may have to accept that I cannot be free.
But all is not lost, life still can be; I still can be.
They cannot take this away from me.
I like this.

Key Points

- Friends are welcome in my building.

- It's OK to need others in my life.

- Its OK if others need me in their lives to help make their plans successful.

- Self-acceptance is the only foundation to build upon. I need to accept other people for who they are too.

- Difference can separate us from one another, or it can bring interest into the building of who we are. This can help to cement it together.

- It is good to explore the building of my life and see what made me who I am. In doing this, I can find uses for failed plans, plans that were unexpected and new plans.

- Routine tends to make completing my plans more possible. If it is not built into the structure of my day, it is not so achievable.

CHAPTER 8

Buildings in need of maintenance and repair

My life might need restorative treatment

Looking after ourselves (maintenance)

I have found looking after myself quite a challenge. It involves many different aspects of care; for example, physical care, emotional care, mental care and social care. Physical care usually involves food, clothing, time, activity, sleep, interests and healthcare. Recently, in fact only this past week, I realised that I can choose whether to eat more food or less food. I found this new understanding quite a revelation! It has released me from the 'need' to eat all of the food placed before me. It has released me from the need to eat when I am actually not hungry. The result is that I am now moving towards an appropriate weight, whereas before I was over the weight that is best for me. Food has been an obsession of mine for most of my life. It isn't that I eat in binge fashion, just that I eat too much too often. I am hopeful that, from now on, I can appreciate my ability to choose and that this will keep me 'on the straight and narrow'. If I move in and out of this understanding, this is OK, it is part of the process of discovery.

Knowing what, where and how to eat can present major problems for some individuals. At times I think that this is connected to difficulties with change or transition. I find it useful to have 'eating times' built into the structure of my day. I think that most of us, whether neurotypical individuals, or individuals with Asperger's Syndrome, also find this helpful. Maybe this is why, in most cultures and societies, we have specific meal times set out for us. For instance, in Western society, we have a time for breakfast, a time for morning tea, lunch, afternoon tea, dinner, supper and so on. Structuring our eating is part of maintaining the building of our life.

Clothing

I find it best to sort my clothing into appropriate apparel for different situations. 'Change' is, again, one of the difficulties that I face with clothing. Knowing what to wear, how and when, is a decision that I don't favour very much, so I attempt to sort it out into 'rules' about things. This means, for instance, that in the spring and summer months I wear clothing that is lighter, less warm than heavier garments, and covers less of my body. For example, I will wear tops with short sleeves instead of tops with long sleeves. However, I am learning not to be completely rigid about this. Sometimes, even though it is summer, the air gets cool and I am allowed to put on a long sleeved top if I wish.

I also have clothing for various occasions; for example, casual clothes for Saturdays at home (actually, for any day at home) and more formal clothes for more formal occasions. I have to tell you, though, that my idea of formal and your idea of formal might be different! I'm not a person who likes 'dressing up'. I do enjoy putting on my 'best' pants and a 'good' shirt with my 'presenting' shoes whenever I present a lecture at seminars or workshops. However, I'm not into suits, dresses, skirts or make-up! Coming to terms with who I am, what I like to wear and when I should wear it, is a process I'm still working on. At times I feel intimidated by others and the knowledge that they seem to have about these things. However, I'm getting better at accepting 'me'. This is a journey that can take a long time, I think. I'm in it for the long haul, are you?

Sometimes I need to buy new clothes, new shoes and other new bits and pieces. I like the idea of new things. I like the idea of looking at new things and, lately, I have actually liked to go out shopping for new things. However, coping with the potential change that this might mean is often difficult. Just this week I have been wearing the new shoes that I bought over a year ago. For more than a year these shoes sat neatly under my bed. I looked at them now and then; I realigned them, when, after vacuuming the carpet they sat upon, they got moved about. I even bought insoles for them, but I never wore them. Eventually my beloved ancient trainers became just too 'tatty' and let the water in when it rained. I felt very uncomfortable about wearing my new shoes. I tried them on and just walked around the house with them on. Then I said to myself 'It's time to let the old shoes go. It's time to wear the new shoes now'. It wasn't easy or comfy to do this, and at first the new shoes felt strange on my feet. They were not uncomfortable, just different. Now, however, over a week later, the new shoes don't feel so strange and I am very happy in them!

I think that many changes and transitions can be encountered as difficult. This applies to neurotypical individuals as well. I think we probably encounter them differently, though. For neurotypical individuals, facing the everyday challenge of change and/or transition can be exciting. Sometimes it is a welcomed event, a time for new things, new adventures and new possibilities. For many of us, as individuals with Asperger's Syndrome, change may mean discomfort, suspicion, confusion and fear. This is perfectly reasonable. When we haven't experienced a particular thing before, how can we know that it will be all right? How can we trust that the outcome will be a good one? Well, the good news with clothing, anyway, is that it is fine to get used to new things slowly. It is fine to think you like something and then change your thinking and decide you don't like it after all. It is fine to explore how particular clothes make you feel. I understand that even neurotypical individuals often do this.

Time

The seconds seem to tick away,
As there goes the end of another day.
Did I do all I wanted to?
Did I say what I needed to?
Will I get time to revisit this day?
Can I regain what I lost on the way?
Will time keep my secrets, safe and sound,
Or will I discover that they have been found?

I waste so much time in my fear of 'the time',
I lose so much joy with stress in my mind.
Oh to relax and appreciate 'Time'.
Oh to know 'Safe', please throw me a line.

I've given you 'Time' Wendy.'
Tis there for your needs.
I want you to recognise all of its seeds.
Using them wisely allows 'time' to grow.
Take 'time' to wander.
Take 'time' to know.

Time can be a welcome asset to all of us. When someone is trying to hurry me up I just get more flustered and confused. I don't think this is a good use of time. It might work for some of our neighbours, and that is fine, but for us this is not the best idea. You and I may even need to allow extra time. If someone says it takes them half an hour to get ready for some event, I probably need an hour. I may not use all of that time, but it is better for me if I am not hurried and I have a longer amount of time to process the events that are occurring.

I really value structured time, rather than 'free' time. I think that many neurotypical individuals feel the same way but often haven't realised it. For example, I notice that they often use diaries and write down their appointments. I assume that they do this because they also like to know what they can expect to happen in their day. I know that people often speak about 'free' time and value space away from demand. However, again, I have noticed that even this time they plan for! I'm sure there are times when some individuals choose to do something, 'on the spur of the moment' (suddenly, without planning it, because they fancy it). For these individuals, these times are often very pleasant and enjoyable. We are all different and this is OK.

Moods and emotions

Being governed by hormones, our moods and emotions are often very changeable. Hormones are enzymes or chemicals that our bodies produce to enable us to carry out particular tasks. They are often the trigger that leads to our bodies doing other things. For instance, when we feel afraid, our bodies produce a hormone called adrenalin. This then enables our muscles to act quickly so we can either run away from perceived danger, or stay and fight. This reaction is often called the 'fight or flight' response. Of course hormones govern so many other things that happen to us. In fact, they trigger every chemical reaction in our bodies.

This is one reason why it is important to have a balanced diet. Eating lots of fruit, vegetables, complex carbohydrates, fish and other proteins, keeping salt and saturated fats to a minimum, and drinking plenty of water, helps our bodies to function effectively. If my diet is too limited and I'm not eating enough of a variety of fruit and vegetables, I notice that my moods are more negative than positive. I also am more inclined towards constipation and this is telling me that I need more fibre in my diet. Moods and emotions are also influenced by my intake of appropriate minerals and vitamins. I am inclined towards depression when my diet is inadequate in iron, vitamin C, the 'B' group of vitamins and vitamin E. This is personal to me of course, but it might apply to others too. It cannot do any harm to check this out for yourself, if you feel the need to.

Another factor that influences our moods and emotions is our general state of 'wellbeing'. Feeling good about who I am, what I do and where I fit into this world of ours, are vital factors in my feeling confident and able. If my self-esteem is low, my mood might be low too. Maintaining my building will involve regular and appropriate eating patterns, exercise and building a positive self-image of who I am and what I do.

Sleep

Neurotypical individuals appear to need to sleep between 6 and 8 hours a night. Maybe this is the case for you as a person with Asperger's Syndrome? I think, at times, it might be nice to have that amount of sleep, but usually this is not the way it is for me. I tend to find getting off to sleep very difficult and staying asleep very difficult too. I frequently wake every hour throughout the night and, on a good night, I sleep for four hours only. Of course, the plus for me is that I get lots of opportunity during the quietness of night-time to work at my computer. If you are a person who longs for sleep but finds this difficult to achieve, the following might work for you. I know many neurotypical individuals who use these.

- Restrict your drinking of tea and coffee throughout the day. Don't drink either of these fluids after 5pm. Limit alcohol to one average glass only (one beer or one wine).

- Eat small meals often. For example, breakfast, then a fruit snack two hours later. Lunch, then a healthy snack two hours later. Eating something reasonable every three hours throughout the day is better than bingeing at night. If we eat close to the time we retire to bed, our stomachs will be working overtime and this could interfere with rest.

- Avoid watching dramatic shows on television that end late at night. These can fuel your imagination and make it difficult to 'switch off'.

- If you worry about forgetting things you need to do, have a pen and paper beside your bed that you can use to write things down as they come to mind.

- Sometimes I find that I need to talk about things that are going on in my head before I can sleep. I might find it useful to do this, like debriefing, into a cassette tape-recorder. At times I can access a good friend and we can talk through things together. This is only for reassurance, and not a time to get into any 'heavy' or difficult conversation.

- Maybe you would find it helpful to read? Some people I know find reading a book that interests them a good way to become sleepy. I find it does the opposite for me, but we are all different.

- I like to sleep with a pouch of dried lavender near or under my pillow. Some individuals would find this uncomfortable because they don't like 'fragrant' things.

- A glass of water near your bed may be good. Just knowing it is there can be helpful.

- Eating a small snack (banana, a piece of bread or toast) may also help.

Interests and hobbies

Being able to give my time to things that I enjoy is very important. I think this is true for all of us. I know that sometimes it is very difficult to be motivated towards anything. At times the things I am interested in are difficult for other people to relate to. So, even though I am completely taken up with an interest of mine and long to tell someone about it, I need to check in with them first. That is, I need to ask them if they are interested in hearing about it. If they are not interested and don't want to join me in conversing about my interests, maybe I can listen to them share about something they are interested in? The other thing we could do is reschedule for another time to get together when they might be interested in sharing with me, my interests, and/or theirs.

At times I have found it difficult to motivate myself, even when I have been interested in a particular subject or activity. This lack of motivation is usually based in my not being able to access the process of actuating that interest; for example, I might not know how or where to begin. I might not know how to implement the steps towards an activity even when I know what the steps are. It is useful and part of caring for ourselves, to be able to ask for assistance at such times.

My life seemed to take a wrong turn. Please help me find the right road again

Asking for assistance

At times, knowing that we need assistance may be difficult to appreciate and work out. I may simply feel uncomfortable or even angry, but not know the reason. I may think that other individuals in my life ought to know that I need help, and be waiting for their support. Usually, however, because neurotypical individuals usually don't have a problem in knowing that they need help, they might not appreciate that it could be a difficulty for us. We need to let them know that we are feeling uncomfortable and even gain their (a good friend's) assistance in seeking out why and what might be good to do about it. It might simply be a matter of structuring. This means a process of setting out and ordering the necessary steps towards accomplishing what it is we need or want to be doing.

Taking care of our health

All of these things are contributors to good health: eating appropriately, getting enough sleep, being able to enjoy what we do, being able to draw upon the help of others and so on. I have often heard the word 'independence' bandied about as if it were some special place to get to. I think I am already a very independent person. It is learning how to be interdependent and share resources with others that I find the most difficult. Neurotypical individuals are often quite good at this and learning from them could be useful to us. There are many agencies that exist to help with supporting the needs of the community; we are part of the community. Some of these agencies are connected to medical needs. For example, we have medical centres, dental and orthotics centres, community centres, chiropractors, physiotherapy centres and so on. These centres exist for the use of all individuals. They want us to make use of the services that they offer.

As we can see from all of the above, maintenance and replenishment of our building takes a bit of thought and planning; this is also true of repairs. Any building gets worn in places and will need to get fixed up at times. It is the same for the building that is our body and our soul. In some ways, caring, repairing and maintaining our physical body is simpler than looking after our emotions, our spirit, our soul; the person we are on the inside. At times this aspect of who we are gets neglected.

I try to take things one at a time, but lately everything comes at once

Our soul

Part of looking after who I am on the inside involves following pursuits that give me 'life', that nourish who I am and that give me a sense of satisfaction. For me this might mean using some time to read, talk to a good friend, write poetry and make lists, listen to music, walk in parks and along the beach and watch videos. I don't do all of these all of the time, just some of them some of the time. I will feel like doing different things at different times. For example, I won't always feel like listening to music. At times I value the silence of no words and no music, just the sounds of the birds and the wind in the trees. Looking out over the ocean or over a river really makes me feel good. Even when I feel life is being unkind or unjust, I can gain a sense of 'I'm OK' whilst looking out over the water. What does this for you?

Do you have something in your life that just makes you feel good? It really is important to nourish your soul. If we use all of our time to take care of material things, but neglect the essence of who we are, our life source will suffer and our building could become a cold and unwelcoming place. Yes, even a place where we ourselves don't want to be.

Repairs

When it comes to taking care of any repairs that the building of our life requires, we will want to check out that we have the right materials for the job. First we need to decide what areas in our building require attention. Is it to do with the foundations? Is it the walls or the wall coverings? Is it the electrics or the plumbing? Once we have established what repairs need doing and where, we can decide upon when and how.

What might be some guidelines that we could use? Well, we could use the guidelines that we apply when we have need of a contractor in real life. The first rule is, always use a qualified person for the job. If you have some concerns about the foundations of your building, you need a builder, not an electrician.

Once you have established the builder's credentials, you could take a look at some of the work they have carried out (completed) for some others. You could even check with previous customers, the owners or occupiers of a building that has been repaired by that builder, to see if they were satisfied with the builder's work. Then you might obtain quotes from different builders, so you could compare proposed work details and costs. The last detail might be a personal one; how do you feel on the inside with these contractors? Do you feel comfortable? Do they listen to your needs? Are they willing to take time with you to explore the best way to do the job? If you don't feel confident with a contractor, it might be best not to choose that one to work for you.

The guidelines above we apply to having someone to work for us on our 'real' buildings; they ought also to apply to the metaphorical building repairs of our other building – ourselves. For example, page 40 outlines some of the qualities we are looking for in a good friend. Sometimes we can gain access to a paid support person who fits the criteria too. I remember being angry that some of the friends that helped me were from an agency; I didn't choose them, they were chosen for me. But, I have to admit that they were able to be a friend and, even if it was only for a short time, they fulfilled a purpose for me and I valued them very much.

Whatever is going on for us, we just need to check people out before we share ourselves with them. For example, is the person I am considering of good reputation? Is this their area of expertise? How well known are they? Do they have a satisfied clientele? What are their fees? Will they commit to me? Do they have a firm under-standing of individuals with Asperger's Syndrome? I need to check out their credentials!

I also need to make a checklist of potential repairs that I think I might need. To keep repairs down to a minimum, it is a good idea to check in with oneself on a regular basis, rather than let things go on and on. Some proverbs about this are: 'A stitch in time saves nine'; 'Better be safe than sorry' and 'Don't put off until tomorrow what you can do today'. All of these imply that we save ourselves from wasted time and energy if we tackle situations whilst they are not too big and 'out of hand'!

Key Points

- I can choose how to care for the building of my life.

- My clothing needs may change. This is OK. I can even buy new clothes if I need to. Sometimes my building needs a new look!

- I need to structure my time to get the best out of it. I may even need to structure my free time.

- My moods and emotions will have an influence upon the building of my life. I can help to create a positive influence by choosing carefully what I eat, how often I exercise, by getting enough sleep and by giving myself space for interest and leisure activities.

- My health is very important to the building of my life. I should not neglect it.

- Nourishing my soul is crucial in creating my building as a place where I can dwell safely and in comfort.

- When it comes to needing to repair parts of the building of my life, I need to get the right materials and attend to this quickly and not allow any damage to worsen.

CHAPTER 9

Revisiting my plans and seeing where they lead me

Are these plans still appropriate?

Reviewing my building plans and taking notice of where they've led me, what changes I had to make along the way and what these changes taught me, is a good strategy for future building plans and actions. As I put strategies into practice, I'll feel more confident with them and with what I hope to gain from them.

'Practice makes perfect' or so they tell us. I'm not sure that this saying is accurate, but I do know that the more often I do something, the more familiar it becomes and the more comfortable I feel about it. If we practise the things we need to learn in life I think it will mean that many of life's processes and decisions become strategies that we can access when we most need them. It's a bit like the need to use our muscles in order to help keep our body strong.

At the end of the last chapter we thought about the building of our life and how to maintain it, repair it or even change our focus of direction. We talked about making and keeping a journal so we could see the problems we might have encountered, where they led us and what this had meant to us. This adds to our overall 'life' concept, or conception. I find that this can be very helpful and can assist us in gaining a picture of who we are, what we want and how other individuals fit into our lives.

Mistakes, misfortunes and misgivings

Learning from our mistakes can be a tricky business! I so often don't make associations from one situation with another, so learning from what went wrong can be very difficult. When I write things down or record them in some way, I can use those recorded events to help me reflect upon what happened. I can then take those reflections, think about them and even explore how they might apply to other events in other areas of my life. I like to think of this as 'plans for everyday living'. I don't think that writing words is the only way to do this, though. You might find it more useful to record events by speaking into a tape recorder, by videoing yourself talking about things, or by sharing with another individual and asking them to take notes for you. Finding the process that suits you best is important. We are all different and may use different ways of noting our experiences.

So This is Life

Stagnant cool unprotected.
An endless ocean of non-entity.
Shapeless visions graying in a colorless void.
Light dominates the passivity of my reflection.
Feeling, many feelings, linking up but not with each other.

Aggression, hate, love, indifference.
Which one and when?
Is it now I'm supposed to respond, or was it yesterday?
'Would you like a bag, Wendy?' What is 'like'? How can I
know?
The moments of time aren't on my side. So little time, and
Decisions need to be made. All the silence tells me is
'Nothing'.

You follow me, seeking, always seeking. You are like
shadows, empty shadows.
What should I wear? Who am I today?
Which one should I be? How to decide. Can't decide.
Chaos, confusion – too many choices!
Feeling lost.

Retreat; soft, gentle, warm. Everything still.
Green, fading into distant mist. Divided into hills, trees,
nothing.
Touching the blue, grey, sky. Unbroken; heat, muzzy,
stormy.
Breeze, soft, gentle warm. Everything still.
All the people have gone. The decisions have left.

At times, making an appropriate decision needs to be based upon
information. This information may be accessible from some past
event we have already experienced. It may be available from another
individual's experience. This is one reason why we share our
thoughts, ideas and hopes with others. Mutual 'planning' or sharing

can be very helpful because it increases our repertoire of opportunity and adds to our ideas about decisions.

Of course there are times when I need to be on my own and explore my thoughts by myself. I might still value sharing these with a good friend at another time, but first I need to gain an understanding of what I might want or need. I don't know about you, but at times I find decision-making overwhelming. I know that at such times I need to give myself some space and 'switch off' for a while. I can come back to the decision plans when I feel I have more energy and can focus upon them. I also need to reassure myself that often there is more than one 'right' decision and it's OK to take my time over this.

Strategies

A strategy is a learned behaviour that we can use when we need to. There are strategies for all sorts of occasions. Neurotypical individuals use them as well. They assist us in our relating to others, as well as in things we do for ourselves. Working out a *structure* for our daily living needs is a strategy. I like to go to bed late and wake up early. I plan to have my breakfast about 7:30, then I get into the other plans for that day. I often organise or structure my days in advance. This allows me to be less anxious about an activity and what it might require, because I have planned for it. Sometimes unplanned events occur and potentially this is very problematic. However, I have a few strategies for when things don't go according to plan!

Interruptions

I may be really focussed upon an event, action or thought when the phone rings or there is a knock on my door. This is very distressing. It is even worse when someone within my household calls out my name and wants me to attend to them for something. I have some strategies for dealing with these times that include the following:

First, these interruptions are allowed, so it's a waste of energy to be angry with them (this kind of anger can hurt me and I don't want that). Second, I am allowed to decide how I'll deal with them. When I'm really needing to focus, I can put the answering machine on to take telephone calls; I can either leave a message on the machine to ask the caller to phone me back at a stated time, or I can say that I'll ring them when I am ready. For people who might call over, I can put a notice on my door saying, 'Please Do Not Disturb', and take it down again when it is convenient for me to answer the door. With regards to my family, I can let my household know that I am not to be interrupted. If music or the television is an intrusion, I can use my ear plugs and ask for the sound to be kept at a reasonable level, not too loud but loud enough! Now, at times it might be really vital that I attend to a specific call. So, if someone still knocks or calls my name, it might be an emergency and I need to attend to that call.

The above are my strategies for coping with interruptions at home. What about interruptions outside of home? Again, because I cannot control others, I cannot control what interruptions might occur. It might be traffic sounds, people's voices, bells, sirens, squeaks, movement and so on. These are all allowed. I can only control me. In order for me to keep control though, I need some rules for myself. It's best that I don't stay amongst crowds or lots of activity for too long a period of time. I get overloaded very quickly and then I can't process things properly. So, I try to aim for shorter periods of time. I make my lists of outside activities and then attempt to execute them in as little time as possible. If someone speaks to me, I reply briefly with a 'hello', but keep moving. Usually other individuals know this as a signal that I don't have time to stop and talk. If, however, someone does persist, I stop, say I'm busy and explain that I'll chat at another time, or that they can phone me to catch up later. It might be an emergency, so again I may need to check out why I'm being called or stopped.

These interruptions are only 'interruptions'. I have my lists; I can get back to what I was doing before I was interrupted. If my thought was interrupted, however, I accept that it will come back to me later, if I cannot reconnect to it straight away. I used to panic over these events. This just makes matters worse for all of us. Neurotypical individuals often don't realise how interruptions affect us. Mostly this is because interruptions don't have the same impact upon them, so it is hard for them to sympathise with us. They do, however, go through times when they don't want to be interrupted either, so they can identify with us at these times. For example they may be watching a favourite show, concentrating upon a difficult task or needing some quiet time.

We might need all kinds of different strategies for a variety of events. We need social strategies, business strategies, family strategies, relationship strategies, shopping strategies and so on. Learning to work out what we should do in what situations can be very difficult, but it is possible. Maybe you could explore what works for you? Try writing down or discussing these. I like plans for possibilities, potentials and profitable interactions. They can help us locate all kinds of hidden ideas we didn't know existed!

Activity

Planning what activities I can and cannot do is very important to me. I know that I cope best when I'm in control and when I'm not amongst large groups of people. So, I plan to travel by car wherever possible, get to places when they are the least busy, shop early, get home early and have only minimal interaction with others. This is called 'taking care of myself'. If I do have to use public transport, then I try to sit in the front of the bus or train, on a single seat if I can, get off promptly and walk on to my destination. If someone does speak to me I respond politely with a brief statement, 'Hi, I'm not in a talking mood just now. Need some quiet, thanks for saying Hi, though'. Then I look the other way. This is a signal to the other person that I am now finished with talking.

Sometimes, I like to visit the cinema. Again I plan this event, get there early so I can choose my seat (usually near an exit), take my refreshments with me so I don't need to queue up for them (or buy them whilst there isn't a queue) and leave as soon as the movie is over. I love to walk near my home. I aim to walk when I know there are likely to be fewer people. This might mean early in the morning and later in the day.

Whatever the activity involves, I try to plan for it. I know that plans don't always work out the way we hope, but we can plan for that too. I tell myself that it is OK if plans are not exactly how I would like them. On my plan I have alternative strategies and alternative possibilities for these events. These can be fun to plot and plan. I hope you enjoy working these into your daily life as much as I do.

Key Points

- It is good to review the plans for the building of my life. I can see what strategies work and which ones need some improvement.

- Keeping up a journal or some form of written record will assist me in learning from past choices.

- Frequently putting into practice the strategies and lessons I have learnt will help to keep them fresh in my mind and keep my building firmly established.

- Mistakes are not always a bad thing. Sometimes they can be useful in our buildings as they show us things we might otherwise have missed.

CHAPTER 10

Being comfortable and satisfied with our building

I have often commented about our being different to one another. Accepting 'difference' isn't always easy but I think it is a very necessary part of any successful living strategy. If my building is to be a safe dwelling place for me, and one that others can safely visit, then understanding that we are all different and have different needs, wants, likes, hopes and dreams is essential. In order to accept others, though, I must first accept myself. I know that this can be a difficult process. Accepting oneself does not mean liking everything about who we are. I don't always like aspects of 'me'. Some of who I am I wish I were not! I don't like being clumsy around others. I don't like how I lose words when I'm struggling to make conversation. I don't enjoy feeling like an idiot in some situations that most people take for granted as being 'easy'. However, accepting my diffability as part of the package I come in, makes my life much easier to deal with. I'm not suggesting that we use Asperger's Syndrome as an excuse for not doing things, just that we aim at being 'inclusive' towards ourselves, as well as towards others.

Wendy

Fair skinned and freckled, podgy, pedantic and particular, that's me.
Dark hair, not so tall, I need glasses to help me see.
I rescue beetles, ants and spiders,
I love water, shades and 'Sliders'.
Science fiction, books about nature, birds, butterflies and bush.
Pussy cats, dogs, sunshine and rainbows,
These are the things that turn me to mush.

I don't like mathematics; numbers make me hurt.
Can't trust me with money or leave me with the purse.
I'll work it all out; sort of. Get there in the end.
But in the meanwhile there is this trend,
Wendy loses another friend.

I'm good at the things I do so well.
But, 'Oh dear' with the things I do not.
I'm clumsy, hyperactive and find it hard to tell,
That the time has come to stop.
'I must sort this now'. I can't go to sleep'.
'Oh yes you must. Now, not another peep.'

> I toss and I turn all through the long night.
> I want sleep to come but it's far out of sight.
> So, up I get once more to turn my computer on.
> If I cannot sleep in bed I'll not stay,
> But I can write throughout this next day.

Accepting our limitations as well as our strengths is the only way to go. I know I'm not good at everything, but I'm not bad either. In fact, just like everyone else, I'm a mixture of both! I am happy to ask for support when I need it and to offer my support to others who might benefit from some of the things I can do well. Life is like a two way street; we cannot travel in both directions at once, but we can pass one another in our journeys. Our passing can be smooth, enjoyable and rewarding or it can be dangerous, tortuous and painful. I prefer the first one, how about you? If we are courteous to one another, learn from each other and show care and consideration on our travels, I believe we will experience some very good things. There is a saying, it's a metaphor: 'what goes around, comes around'. I think it means that whatever we give out to others we can expect to receive back. This is not so much to do with material things, though, as it is with matters of care and concern.

What kind of self-portrait would you paint of yourself? How well do you know yourself? Do you like who you are? What do other people say about you? If you are unsure about these points maybe you could check them out.

The building of your life

I hope by now you will have some understanding of the life you are building. When you reflect safely upon your past, I hope that it will help you understand your future. Do your plans enable you to cross over into the territory of another? If so, do you know how to encounter them? Most neurotypical individuals don't seem to need a plan to help them know what relationship is appropriate for which people in their lives. They seem more internally connected to others and able to work these things out. However, they don't always get it right all of the time. Yes, even those polytropic individuals who are able to use divided attention get it wrong too. So, planning the building of our lives and exploring how we want them to be gives meaning and understanding to a chaotic world. We could probably all benefit from doing this.

My daily planner

Which bits do we include for now and which bits do we look at later?

I remember one young woman who explained that she couldn't be employed and be in a relationship with a man. She chose to give up her job and work on her romantic relationship. I don't know if she was successful; I just find it interesting to note that she found it impossible to be involved in both things at once. Some people can do many different things and still have the energy for more! I'm more likely to be able to have a few things happening for me, but not attend to them all at the same time. I give my attention to my writing on one day. The next day I do some domestic house-work. The day after this

I go for walks, do some shopping and some reading. I have found, at times, that I can structure the day into specific segments and areas, which allow me to focus upon one event at any one time. This way I get several activities into one day. However, I cannot maintain this for very long. Maybe you are like me? Maybe your plan looks different? The issue is that you discover what works best for you and your circumstances.

Keeping safe

How does one explore life potential and keep safe at the same time? None of us knows what we may encounter around the next corner. This is true, but we can use some precautions for our time of discovery. For example, whilst working on a building site the workers wear safety hats and steel capped shoes for protection. What safety gear could you wear? What protection will you take as you explore the plans for your building? Well, you could reflect on past encounters that you may have recorded and use what you learnt before as a protective shield for what lies in front of you. You could use 'support' from others as a safety net. You don't need to go it alone. Use the plan that you have created to date; there may be some tips for your future plans. If you are unsure of the terrain ahead, you may be able to check it out first, before you venture out. I have a 'saying' that helps me in my decision processing: 'If in doubt leave it out'. This might be helpful to you too. I always find that it makes life easier when I know what to expect before I get there. In some situations this is easy to do. I can go to a hall, cinema, shopping precinct, street and so on and explore them before I need to use them. When it is quiet and there are no other demands upon me, I can check things out. I can find out where all the entrances and exits are, what the place contains, how big the places are and so on. However, sometimes we just cannot do this and we don't know what we might encounter. This is OK too. I can use what I know from other situations. I can include phone numbers of friends who would help me if I needed them. If I still am not comfortable, I can go back to my building and venture out another day.

Encountering strangers

As we work on the building of our life, we might have encounters with others who we haven't met before. I am always cautious about meeting new people. I don't mind meeting interesting people and I look forward to sharing mutual interest. The difficulty is getting to the place where we each know that this person is interesting and worth sharing with. I'm not so good at 'small talk'. This is the term used by neurotypical individuals for superficial conversation, and may include topics of conversation based around someone's name, employment, living and weather conditions. Apparently most individuals value this as a beginning to getting to know someone. Many individuals feel uncomfortable if this stage is missed. The difficulty for me is that I often forget this and tend to dive into a conversation based upon my factual knowledge about things I'm interested in. For many neurotypical individuals this might seem rude or strange. So, I attempt to go through the stages that most other people are more familiar with. These are:

○   An introduction of oneself (name, employment, where I live and so on). This needs to be kept brief though, only a few sentences, and must be invited from the other person.

○   An invitation for the other person to introduce themselves ('So, how about you? Where are you from?')

○   A mutual invitation to talk more, either now or later.

Learning this process and building upon it is, I think, a good basis for friendships. We can exit at any time and are not bound to any commitment during these early stages; this is true for others too. As a friendship develops, we can shape it together and see where it takes us. I need to know that I can keep safe during this process and I'm in control of what I want every step of the way. In a two way street each individual has these same rights.

Seasons

I have come to appreciate that my building must be able to exist in all weathers. I need to be prepared for whatever a season might bring me.

Many trees in summer look lush, green and inviting. In winter, however, these same trees may look barren, brown and lifeless. This is OK. The trees are the same, just going through a different process that is necessary to their life. So it will be for us at times. Our lives can feel like springtime, full of anticipation and new things. At other times we feel quite cold and wintry. It is perfectly fine to have these times; we all do. If you are like me, you might have times when all you want to do is hide away within your building with a good book! Winter is a time for regaining energy, a time for feeling the need to hibernate a little.

Here, in my home town near the ocean in Western Victoria, Australia, the spring will soon arrive. Already there are daffodils and snowflakes (snowdrops) in local gardens. These springtime flowers bring smiles to many faces and give out the message that winter will soon pass. I think it is the same for us. We get some kind of feeling inside of us that prompts us to move out of our cocoons and explore again. Taking risks and extending our building into unknown territory can be a marvellous adventure. Some might say that this is too hard and they prefer to stay snugly wrapped up and indoors. This makes me feel sad, because if you 'never, never go, you will never, never know'! If you use your maps wisely you can rely upon your past and present experiences to assist you in your future decisions.

Working with the building of who we are

For many of us, being employed outside of our home can be quite demanding. It might work for some individuals if they are self-employed and do not need to take instruction from a 'boss' person, because they are their own boss. However, for others amongst us, following instructions given to us by others can be a nightmare. Quite often neurotypical individuals speak too fast for us to keep up. They may use lots of metaphor and assume that we have the concepts for what they are saying. Unfortunately, we might not be able to fully comprehend all that is required of us and this can lead to difficulties at work. For these types of reasons, working for oneself, and at a place we feel comfortable, can be more productive. Maybe it's the same reason I wasn't so good at school with team sports, but I did well in individual sporting events, such as swimming.

Finding the right occupation for 'you' is very important. You might find it useful to check your plans and see what your skills and talents are, as well as your hopes and dreams. Check in with others and ask them for their opinion about your skills. I love to write and I also enjoy teaching. However, I couldn't work as part of a team at a school or university because of my comprehension difficulties. So, I work from home and I work for myself as a self-employed person. I am fortunate. I have family who support me. Most of my work arrangements take place over the internet and I can record all my appointments on my computer. My partner takes care of accounts and the paper work for me because I would find this too difficult to do for myself. I don't drive a motor-car. This means that I depend upon others to drive me to where I need to go, or I travel by public transport, with arrangements to be met and be taken where I need to go. These things can happen for me because I have good support from my friends and from my family. I know that this might not be available for everyone. The other alternative, of course, is support from an agency that specialises in supporting individuals with disabilities.

However you go about it, you need to be gainfully employed and be enjoying what you do. This is your right.

Time to move on

Have you ever thought to yourself that you have been in this place for long enough now? Maybe it is time to move on? We all feel at home in one place or another and then, as we grow, we get the impression that we would like to be someplace else. Essentially we may have outgrown the room we are in, or maybe our needs have changed. I love to travel. I'm not too keen on being on aeroplanes; I prefer the feel of firm ground beneath my feet. However, I love the excitement of travelling. You might be wondering how this fits with my need for sameness and my dislike of change. Well, I think that I take my 'sameness' with me. I pack a suitcase that has the same clothes in as usual. I follow the same routines as usual and I usually stay with the same people. If I stay in motels and hotels, then I have that organised ahead of time, with someone to meet me and support me during my stay. This way, I get the best from both worlds!

I could choose to stay within my known world and comfort zone. This would be just fine to do. However, for me I think I need to explore and I need my surroundings to be life giving, colourful and interesting. So, finding the right way for this to happen is very important. 'Life is like a box of chocolates', says Forrest Gump. 'You never know what you are going to get'. Well, I like to know what I am going to get, so I buy the box of chocolates that comes with a description of its contents. You can do the same. You can move rooms if you need to. You might just need to do some exploring first and make some decisions about where you want to go, when you want to go and how you will get there.

Wendy's reflections upon some past and present relationships

In the quietness, I have some time and ability to reflect upon past and current relationships. First I note some general observations about myself. Some of these I am uncomfortable with and I wish they were not so. Others, I'm fine about. Learning to accept these things about myself is important, I know. But I still wish some things were, or could be, different.

General observations

Being unsure how I should relate to most other people is uncomfortable. I'm OK with individuals who have a specific role in life (shop person, bus driver, doctor, teacher) but it is quite difficult to know what to say or do with other individuals who do not have such a well-defined role. The reason that I am OK with relating to those whose role is defined, is because if their role is defined then mine is too. For example, in the shop I am the customer. The customer comes to purchase a product, then leaves. It is similar with the bus driver. I board the bus as a passenger, pay my fare, then exit at my destination. When I visit the doctor, I am the patient. I tell the doctor of my health concerns and I listen to his or her advice, then I leave. With the teacher, I am the student. I attempt to listen to the teacher's words, learn and gain knowledge from them; then I leave. With relationships outside of defined roles, I notice I have a strong tendency to create a role for the individual concerned, and for myself. This can be problematic when the individual does not want that role, does not fit the role expectations or seems to 'fit' for a while and then deviates from expectation.

Over attachment

I am not drawn to form attachments to, or converse with, most other individuals that I encounter in my everyday life. However, now and then I meet someone who stirs something inside of me. I don't understand why this happens and I find it very uncomfortable. In the presence of such a person I may feel a mixture of emotions, for example, confusion, distress and pleasure. Being in their presence can cause me physical pain and fear. On the one hand I feel an attraction and a desire to relate to this person, but on the other hand I'm aware of my inadequacies. I think the worst thing is lack of role definition. 'What am I supposed to say, do, and be, around this person?' I tend to obsess about this person and my whole day can be occupied with what might happen if I should see them or if they should talk to me. I have a tendency to form over attachments to such individuals and I can have high expectations of them.

Expectations

I will long to be with this person and find it difficult to understand that they might not want to be with me all of the time. I may eat, sleep and breathe this person; they may not return my attentions. I can take their lack of attentiveness to mean personal rejection. This personal rejection may turn into self-injury or self-loathing. I tell myself that if I could only 'get it right', 'say it right', 'do it right', then this person would want to be with me all of the time too. I think that I could be wrong here. I think my thoughts and beliefs about this situation may be incorrect. You see, even if I did and said all of the right things, another individual has their own life. They have their own fears, inadequacies, agendas and so on. I may not be the reason for everything that occurs in their lives. They may not be able to be whom and what I need, or think I need them to be.

Rachel

Rachel seemed strong, intelligent, assertive and interested in me. She chose my company and shared her problems with me. I liked her and very quickly formed an attachment. This attachment seemed to be the vehicle for much pain. Rachel was often disappointed with me and told me of my faults. I tried constantly to please her and soon an abusive pattern developed. My constant inability to 'get it right' with this relationship, ended in my attempting suicide. Rachel's disgust with me, my choices and my needs, resulted in her ultimate dismissal of me as a worthy friend. This has been a pattern in my life and learning to break free from it has not been easy.

Current friendships

As I write these words I am aware of a battle of a different kind going on inside of me. I have some lovely friends who are loyal and trustworthy. For me the struggle is one of feeling that I don't deserve them. At times I feel only disconnection and even quite 'dead' emotionally as I think of them. When I am absent from them it's as if they don't exist. I am constantly taken up with the 'now' and the moment. My fear is that I am lying to my friends because of my lack of emotional connection. I mean, how can you say you are a friend when you feel so empty? Am I a deceitful person? I seem to either be attached or disconnected, there is nothing in between! The other potential difficulty is that because I have no feeling for them, I might do something that could hurt them. For example, I may forget to send postcards when I'm on holiday. I may not think to phone them or share my life with them. I may form new friendships and be totally taken up with these, forgetting the friends I have elsewhere.

To date I am still unsure what the answer is to my dilemma. I know that, as the song says, 'Love is not a feeling; it's an act of your will', and I aim to live my life by this philosophy. Maybe this is the answer? Maybe, as we each learn to forgive ourselves our inadequacies and forgive others theirs, our actions will impact upon our emotions and vice versa?

I Know

You touched my life, you entered me.
Life will never be quite the same again.
I still hurt inside, I try to hide, I still want you here, at my side.

Letting go of you and ending pursuit,
Is very hard to say.
I look for your affirmation, telling me I am OK.

Knowing love just isn't enough,
Knowing the past is still full of stuff.
Knowing I'll make it, in spite of this pain.
Knowing I'll be OK once again.

There can't actually be a conclusion in this book because our life journeys are on-going. However, there is an end to these writings, just for here and now. You have the power over your own life. I hope that you will use it to discover positive potential possibilities that unlock exciting moments ahead. Please remember you are not alone in your struggles, even when your feelings suggest that you are. Our life plans and experiences will often be different, this is OK. Variety can be the spice of life, enjoy it.

Key Points

- Difference can be attractive when viewed with honesty and acceptance.

- My limitations may help to keep me dwelling safely in my building. If I did not recognise them I might try things that put my building at risk of damage.

- My strengths give my building its character and enable it to stand alongside other buildings.

- There is a time for planning, a time for building and a time for dwelling.

- It is OK to think and plan to move on in the building of your life. You might like a change of scenery!

- Taking in and observing how other people live can be useful. I need to work out what the role of my building is.

- At times roles can become confused and blurry. Relationships can cause us pain. Learning how to let go of crumbling and unsafe relationships can be messy, but it needs to happen!

- Expectations need to adapt with changing environments. However, we need to be gentle with ourselves and build our lives steadily, as we are able, and as we can.

- This is the building of your life. You have charge of it.

Some common metaphors or idioms

Sometimes using a metaphor (saying words that promote emotive connections, but not meaning them literally) is the only way that individuals can express how they feel, what they hope for and/or what they need. I have written down a few common sayings for you. They are under general headings only. If you are interested you can explore them in more detail by chatting about them with a friend or doing your own research about their origins. The important thing is to be aware that people use metaphor and do so because they are emphasising what they want to say. A metaphor for this is: stressing a point!

A light bulb moment – a moment when you suddenly understand

A light came on in my head – I suddenly understood something

A raw deal – bad luck, or to get the worst of a deal

A rough night – didn't sleep very well

A rough road – a time of troubles in life

A rule of thumb – a general rule which applies in many situations

A stiff upper lip – not showing sadness or emotion

A stitch in time saves nine – taking preventative measures; doing something now will save time in the future

A square deal – a fair deal

A square meal – A balanced meal; a big meal; a full meal

All fingers and thumbs – very clumsy

All sewn up – finished, completed

All the bells and whistles – extra embellishments

Ants in her pants – fidgety

As bright as a new pin – clean, new

As fresh as a daisy – not tired, refreshed

As green as grass – naïve, innocent

As nice as pie – very nice, but with an implication that it might not be sincere

As rough as guts (bags) – uncouth, uncultured, bad mannered

As slow as a month of Sundays – very slow and boring

As slow as a wet week – very slow

At the end of my tether – feeling that I just can't stand the situation any more

Bad apple – a person who has bad intentions

Bad cough – a cough that sounds bad; a cough that indicates you are unwell

Bad day – a day when things don't go well

Banging your head against a brick wall – making no progress in solving a difficult problem

Be on your best behaviour – try to be very polite

Beat about the bush – use a lot of unnecessary words to talk about something instead of getting to the point

Begging on hands and knees – begging and pleading for something

Being a bit flaky – acting strangely because of being tired or stressed; being unreliable

Being frank – being completely honest

Belt up – put on your seat belt; be quiet, especially a rude way to tell someone to stop talking

Bent over backwards to help – did everything you possibly could to help somebody

Between a rock and a hard place (on the horns of a dilemma) – having to choose between two unpleasant things or make a difficult decision

Bide your time – waiting for an appropriate time

Bite your tongue – refrain from saying something you really want to say

Biting off more than you can chew – trying to do more than you are capable of doing

Black humour – jokes about sad or upsetting things

Blockhead – somebody stupid

Blow me down – I'm amazed

Blown away – amazed, awed

Break a leg – good luck!

Bright as a button – very smart, clever

Buckle up – do up your seat belt

Building bridges (of friendship) – learning to understand one another

Bundle of nerves – somebody very nervous who worries a lot

Burst into laughter – start laughing suddenly

Bursting at the seams – very full

Bursting with enthusiasm – very enthusiastic

Bursting with happiness – very happy

Burying your head in the sand – refusing to see how things really are

Bushed – exhausted, or lost (in the Australian bush)

Can't see the wood for the trees – focusing on detail rather than the whole picture

Can't you see the light? – can't you understand?

Cat's got your tongue – tongue-tied; too shy to talk

Cheeky – being funny or silly in an incorrigible way

Coming down in sheets – raining heavily

Cried your eyes out – cried a lot

Cry baby – someone who cries a lot; someone who is easily given to crying over issues that to most other people are not upsetting

Cut up about something – upset about something

Dancing to the beat of a different drum – having different motivations to other people

Dead beat – somebody stupid

Deadhead – somebody stupid, with no good things about them

Dead set against it – absolutely opposed to it

Dead slow ahead – go slowly just here

Dickhead – stupid person (an offensive expression)

Dive head first into something – to act without thinking of the possible consequences

Doesn't let his right hand know what the left hand is doing – very secretive in his actions. Implication that this is not with good intentions

Don't get your knickers in a knot – don't panic

Don't get your knickers in a twist – don't panic

Don't hold back – tell the whole story, explain the way things really are; give your all to a situation

Don't let the cat out of the bag – keep a secret

Don't start – don't start complaining

Don't talk with your mouth full – don't talk while you have food in your mouth

Don't water down the situation/conversation – don't add unnecessary details that detract from the main point

Dose yourself to the eyeballs – take lots of medicine; get drunk

Down on your luck – when things are not working out the way you had hoped, or when you have run out of money

Down the drain – a failure, lost

Dragged through the bushes – been through a very difficult time

Drawing conclusions – reaching a conclusion, deciding what the main point is; can imply somebody is making incorrect assumptions

Dressing down – wearing very casual clothes, or not dressing as formally as an occasion requires

Dressing up – wearing clothes that are more formal than casual; preparing to go to a party, out to dinner or to some special occasion. May include make-up for women

Drown your sorrows – drink too much alcohol to try to forget your problems

Dry humour – ironic humour

Earning a crust – to earn your money by working

Eat your words – to admit you are wrong

Everything's gone sour – the whole situation has become bad

Face up to it – admit there is a problem

Faint hearted – to feel scared, afraid

Fast food – food bought from a place that serves you very quickly, e.g. McDonalds; food that is pre-prepared and doesn't take long to get ready to eat

Fed up – sick of something

Feeling blue – feeling sad

Feeling seedy – feeling unwell

Feeling upside down – feeling confused

Finger on the pulse – to know everything that's going on

Fishing for a compliment – saying negative things about yourself in the hope that the other person will contradict you by giving you a compliment

Flattery will get you everywhere – if you flatter me, I'll do whatever you want

Foot in mouth (disease) – always saying tactless things

Fought the good fight, finished the race – did the absolute best you could

Full as a boot – drunk

Full as a goog – have eaten too much

Get a grip – stop messing around; make an effort to be more in control

Get all dolled up – get really dressed up and wear lots of make-up etc

Get into the spirit of the thing - do what everybody else is doing

Get into the swing of it - really get into the event (dancing; partying)

Get on your bike – hurry, or leave now; tell someone to go away; tell someone to make an effort

Get stirred up – get enthusiastic and ready for action

Get this down – swallow this

Get tizzied up – get really dressed up

Get under someone's skin – to annoy somebody

Get your dander up – to get really angry or irritated

Get your hands off – don't touch

Get your skates on – hurry

Get your teeth into it – get involved in something, work hard at something

Getting out of the wrong side of bed – waking up feeling grumpy

Getting the wrong end of the stick – misunderstanding something

Give someone the flick – break up with them, end a relationship (or, dismiss them from their job; give them the sack)

Give someone the shirt off your back – give someone everything you own or going to enormous lengths to help someone

Give you a hand – help you

Go around the houses – use a lot of unecessary words to talk about something instead of getting to the point

Go fish for it – look until you find what you want, or (more common) 'I am not going to give you what you are asking for'

Go for it – act enthusiastically to achieve a goal

Go hell for leather – run very fast (or drive a car very fast)

Go like the clappers – go very fast

Go the extra mile – do something extra to help someone else

Golden handshake – a cash payment to somebody who is leaving a job

Good and ready – to feel that now is the appropriate time

Good egg – a good person

Green with envy – very envious

Had a blast – had a wonderful time

Had a gut full – to be completely sick of something or somebody (or to be drunk)

Had it – very tired (or, 'to have had it with someone' means to be really angry with them)

Had it up to here – to be completely fed up with something or somebody

Halfway to Texas – a very long way

Hang about – wait

Hang on a minute – wait, don't act too quickly

Hard as nails – not showing any feelings

Hard of hearing – going or being deaf; finds it difficult to hear

Have your cake and eat it – want to have everything and not give anything up

He lost it – he got really angry

Heavy hearted – feeling sad or depressed

Heavy load – have a lot of things to worry about

He's a bad penny – he's a bad person

He's a bit wet/he's a drip – he's a bit stupid/naive; lets people bully him

He's a chip off the old block – he's just like his father/mother

He's got a good head on his shoulders – he's sensible and practical

He's/She's my better half – he/she is my husband/wife or romantic partner

High as a kite – drunk or stoned, ie. acting stupidly because of having drunk too much alcohol or taken a mind-altering drug

His bark is worse than his bite – he may sound gruff and grumpy, but really he is quite nice

Hold onto your hat – please wait; don't make a hasty decision; get ready for some turmoil – either physical or emotional

Hold your horses – slow down

Hold your tongue – refrain from saying something

Holding the audience in the palm of your hand – keeping the audience interested so they pay attention to everything you say, or keeping them entertained/amused just the way you want to

Hop to it – get on with it, be quick

Humble pie (eating humble pie) – apologizing

I can't stand for it – I can't tolerate it

I didn't come down in the last shower – I'm not stupid, I know what you're trying to do

I felt like dying – I felt extremely embarrassed, mortified, humiliated, ashamed

I fumbled my way through – I did the best I could but I found it hard

I want to jump your bones – I want to make passionate love to you

I wasn't born yesterday – I'm not stupid, you can't fool me

I'd give my right arm for... - I'd really like to have/do...

I'm not as green as I am cabbage looking – I'm not stupid

I've got butterflies in my tummy – I feel very nervous

If you don't tell me I'll burst – I'm extremely curious about what you are going to tell me and I desperately need to know

In a black mood – feeling sad, down, depressed, angry

In the heat of the moment – at the time when you are feeling very angry or passionate about something

In the poo – in trouble

In the running – has a chance to win a competition

In the soup – in trouble

In the thick of things – being very busy doing things with other people. Being in the midst of the action, whatever it is.

Instant coffee – not instant – you have to boil the kettle; coffee made with granules stirred into boiling water

It all blew up in our faces – something going badly wrong

It snowballed – the situation got worse or more extreme

It takes two to tango – you can't do something by yourself, you both have to want to do it

It's a piece of cake – it's easy

It's been a long day – I've had a lot of things to do and I'm feeling tired

It's in the bag – it's finished, completed

Itchy feet – having an urge to travel

Jump out of my skin – jump because you're startled

Jump to it – be quick

Jumping from the frying pan into the fire – moving from a bad situation to a worse situation, or to one equally bad

Keep it under your hat – keep a secret; don't tell this to anyone

Keep it up – keep on doing what you're doing

Keep the home fires burning – take care of domestic issues

Keep your end up – make an effort; play your part; stay equal with somebody

Keep your eye on it – watch the progress of something

Keep your eyes out – being vigilant

Keep your eyes peeled – being vigilant

Keep your hair on – don't get upset

Keep your mind off it – stop thinking about something bad by thinking of something else instead

Keep your nose clean – don't get into trouble

Keep your nose out of it – don't interfere in somebody else's business

Keep your pecker up – keep your courage up, stay enthusiastic

Kick start the conversation – say something interesting that others can start talking about

Kick the bucket - die

Killing myself laughing – laughing a lot

Knackered – comes from the idea of an elderly horse being no good as a work horse due to being too old and so is given to the butcher (the knacker) 'feeling knackered', old, tired

Knock me down with a feather – I am very surprised

Knocked over – very surprised

Knocked sideways – very surprised/shocked by something

Laughed your head off – laughed uproariously

Leading someone astray – to encourage someone away from what is right

Leading someone up the garden path – leading someone to believe something that isn't the case

Let your hair down – to relax and be casual

Light as a feather – very light

Light hearted – happy, cheerful, joyful

Lighten up – don't be so serious

Like a bat out of hell – very fast

Like a bull in a china shop – clumsy, blundering around

Like a fish out of water – in an unfamiliar situation, or, somebody who doesn't fit in

Like a herd of elephants – causing a great commotion, making a lot of noise

Like death warmed up – looking (or feeling) very sick

Like two peas in a pod – exactly the same as each other, usually in terms of looks

Lily livered coward – a coward

Listen to reason – stop and listen

Liven up – be less serious and quiet; learn to have a laugh

Living life in the fast lane – doing as much as possible in life, going to lots of parties etc

Live life to the full – as above, but with the implication that this is making you happy

Living on love – not feeling like eating because of the intense emotional feelings of being in love

Load of bull – rubbish, nonsense

Look out – be careful

Love makes the world go round – love gives a reason for the good things that happen in the world

Mad as a hatter – completely crazy

Make up your mind – make a decision

Mind over matter – you can change how you feel about something by thinking positive thoughts

Mind the step – don't trip or fall down the step

Mind your manners – be polite

Mum's the word – I won't tell anybody what I've just been told

My heart nearly jumped out of my chest – I got a terrible fright

My mind's gone blank – I can't remember something

My/your other half – my or your spouse

Nail biting finish – a tense ending

No hoper – somebody who doesn't seem able to succeed in life

Not playing with a full deck; A few bricks short of a load; To have toys in the attic; a sandwich short of a picnic; not the full quid – all of these mean mentally defective or very stupid

Now you've gone and done it – now you've messed something up

Off colour – unwell

Off with the fairies – day dreaming

Old fart – an old person with fixed ideas

On a downer – things are bad and getting worse

On a roll – good things keep happening

On the up and up – things are getting better

One for the road – have just one more drink before you leave

Out of sight – really excellent, amazing

Out of sorts – not in a very good mood or not feeling very well

Over the hill – old, no longer capable of working hard

Over the top – extreme

Pale as a ghost – to have a very pale face, usually because of a fright

Pick up your feet – move faster

Pins and needles – tingling sensation in one's limbs

Pitchforked into something – suddenly have to do something you don't want to do, or had not expected to do

Pointed remark – a remark that implies something about someone, usually something not very nice

Pressing needs – needs that need to be met urgently

Pull your socks up – make more of an effort, do better

Pull yourself together – do better or stop being emotional and be rational.

Push off – leave

Put them in their place – show someone that they are wrong about something

Put up a good fight – to do your very best in a difficult situation

Put up a good front – to pretend everything is all right when it isn't really

Put up or shut up – do something about a situation or stop complaining about it

Put your best foot forward – do your best

Put your money where your mouth is – be prepared to support your words with actions, to act on what you believe

Put your weight behind it – put all your effort into something

Put your whole self into it – do a task very enthusiastically, as well as you can

Raining buckets – Raining very heavily

Raining cats and dogs – Raining very heavily

Really gets my goat – really annoys/irritates me

Red as a beet – to be blushing, to have a red face, to be embarrassed

Ring any bells? – does this remind you of something?

Roundabouts and swings – different things in life amount to the same in the end

Rub me up the wrong way – irritate me

Run like mad – run very fast

Run of the mill – ordinary

Run with it – develop an idea

Scared to death – extremely scared

See sense – understand what a proper course of action would be

Self-made man – someone who has become successful without anybody else's help

Setting each other off – causing each other to act in certain ways

She'll be apples – everything will be all right

She'll be right – it will all turn out all right in the end

She's all front – what she says is not the same as what she does

She's all over the place – she's disorganised

She's sending out signals – she's showing that she's attracted to somebody

She's scatty – she's disorganised

She thinks she's the ant's pants – she feels really good about herself

Shedding some light on the subject – make it more understandable; explaining

Shitting bricks – very frightened

Shop till you drop – go on a shopping spree

Sick as a dog – very sick

Sick joke – a joke that some people would not find funny or would be upset by

Sing for it – do something to earn what you want

Sit down and sit up – pay attention

Sit on it – don't tell anybody else a piece of information you know

Slapstick – practical jokes

Sleep it off – to expect to feel better about something after sleeping

Smarty pants – someone who seems to know everything

Soft in the head – stupid, not sensible

Someone's gone all soft – they're not showing much sense

Spice up your life – add something interesting to your life, do something you enjoy

Spitting chips – very angry

Squeaky clean – completely honest and trustworthy

Stand by me – support me when I need it, usually in expectation of trouble to come

Star gazing – day dreaming

Starving to death – extremely hungry

Steady as she goes – continue slowly and patiently

Stick in the mud – someone who doesn't want to change or accept new ideas

Stick to your guns – be firm about something

Sticky beak – someone who wants to know everybody else's business

Stop playing games – stop being devious

Strike me dead – how surprising

Strike me pink – I'm very surprised

Stripped naked – laid bare; uncovered; to have nothing to hide

Strong as an ox – very strong

Stuffed – eaten too much; made a big mess of something; out of energy

Switched on – knowing what's happening

Take a moment – pause for a moment

Take a punt – take a chance; gamble

Take a shower – have an all over wash under the shower

Take the Mickey – try to trick someone by making them believe something that isn't likely to have happened; tease someone

Taking it as far as it can go – finishing something completely

Taking stern measures – being strict to control a situation

Talk the hind leg off a donkey – to be extremely talkative

Talking frankly – being completely honest

Tearing a strip off somebody – telling somebody that you are very angry with them

That makes me sick – that makes me feel disgusted

That's a tall order – that will be hard to achieve or do

That's dear – cost a lot; expensive

That's my bread and butter – that's my way of financially supporting myself

That's torn it – now everything has gone wrong

The cat's pyjamas – wonderful

The cat's whiskers – the best

The green-eyed monster - jealousy

The light is on, but nobody's home – this person just isn't connecting with what I am saying; this person has a very low IQ

The long and the short of it – the whole story

The moving finger of time – the fact that time passes

The night is young – it's not very late yet, so we still have time to have a good time

The shit hit the fan – 'Now we really are in trouble'

The sparks were flying – they were having a fight or argument

The thin end of the wedge – if this particular thing happens, it opens the way for worse things to happen

There was a spark between them – they felt attracted to each other

There you go – give someone something; you can do it

Thick as a brick – stupid

Thick as two short planks – stupid

Think outside the square – think laterally; think outside of the immediate; being imaginative

Thinking alike – having the same approach to a subject as another person

Ticked off – told off; fed up with, to have had enough off

Tickle your fancy – amuse; spark your interest

Time drags – times seems to pass slowly

To add fuel to the fire – to increase the problem

To be all at sixes and sevens – to feel confused and upset

To be boiling mad – to be extremely angry

To be framed – falsely accused based on fabricated evidence

To be frayed around the edges – not behaving in the usual way, stressed

To be hemmed in – to feel that there is no escape or no solution to a problem

To be informed – to be put in the picture; told the complete state of affairs

To be knocked up – pregnant; tired; beaten up

To be old beyond your years – someone who seems very wise or mature although they are young

To be on the ball – to pay attention to what is going on

To be on the boil – full of enthusiasm

To be on the fast track – to be very successful and be often promoted; city worker; white collar worker

To be on the same wave length – to understand each other completely

To be puffed up – to feel proud of your achievements

To be short changed – to be treated unfairly

To be short of time – to have too many things to do in a given time

To be short on patience – to be impatient

To be spot on – to be exactly right about something

To be starry eyed – to be very happy because of being in love; to be naïve

To be too big for your boots – to feel proud when you don't really have anything to be proud of

To be up yourself – to feel proud, to brag about your own accomplishments

To beat your own drum – to praise yourself

To bite off more than you can chew – to try to do something before you have learnt how to do it

To blow a fuse – to get extremely angry

To blow your own whistle/trumpet – to praise yourself

To buttonhole somebody – to stop somebody and keep talking to them

To cry buckets – to cry a lot

To cry on someone's shoulder – to tell someone all your troubles

To cry wolf – to give a false alarm to trick people into thinking you need help

To defuse the situation – take the pressure off, change the subject

To draw the short straw – to be unlucky; to have to do what nobody else wants to do

To drown one's sorrows – drink (alcohol) to forget life's problems

To earn your stripes – prove yourself worthy of reward, respect

To eyeball somebody – to stare at somebody (may or may not be malicious)

To face the music – to know you're going to get into trouble and accept it

To fade with time – memories become less clear as time passes

To fall for someone – to feel intense love for someone

To fall in love – to suddenly feel intense love for someone

To fan the flames – to do things which cause your feelings of love to intensify; to make an emotional situation more intense

To feel pinned down – to feel unable to escape from a situation/person

To gather your wits – to think carefully about something

To gather your thoughts – to think carefully about something and not think about the consequences

To get belted up – put on your seat belt; also can mean to be hurt or by someone who punches you

To get carried away – to get very enthusiastic about something

To get on like a house on fire – to be really good friends with someone

To get on the wrong side of someone – to make a bad impression, to make someone dislike you

To get up your nose – to be very annoying/irritating

To get warmed up – to gradually become enthusiastic about something

To get on your high horse – become/feel offended. Retaliate in your defence

To give someone the finger – tell somebody to go away in a rude and forceful way

To hang in there – wait patiently for a desired outcome, keep working toward a goal

To hang out together – to spend time together

To hang up your hat – stop trying; you can stay here

To have a broken heart – to feel extremely sad about a love affair that has ended.

To have a chip on your shoulder – to feel angry with everybody all the time for no apparent reason. Also, to be bitter or resentful about something, which negatively affects your interactions.

To have a one track mind – to think about only one subject all the time, often used to imply that somebody is thinking about sex all the time

To have a slice of the action – be involved in something

To have wandering hands – to touch somebody in inappropriate places

To have your head screwed on the right way – to be sensible

To have your mind in the gutter – to be thinking about sex

To keep mum – to keep a secret

To keep on his good side – to try to please someone

To keep your eye on the ball – watch the progress of something

To keep your wits about you – don't get disturbed by a chaotic or unusual or dangerous situation

To kick a man when he's down – do something bad to someone when he's already had a lot of bad luck

To know where someone's coming from – to understand why someone thinks in a certain way or has certain opinions

To live by your wits – to be smart

To lose one's train of thought – to forget what you were going to say, or forget the point of what you are saying, in the middle of saying it

To make a long story short – to just tell the main point

To paddle your own canoe – to act independently

To pick up the pace – move or work faster

To play chicken – to see who opts out of a dangerous game first

To play dead – to not respond

To point the finger – to accuse somebody of something

To pull someone's leg – to try to make someone believe something that isn't true or that is impossible

To pull the wool over someone's eyes – to trick or deceive someone

To pull your finger out – stop messing around and get to work

To pull yourself up by your shoelaces – improve your situation entirely by your own efforts

To put the hard word on someone – threaten somebody with bad consequences if they don't do something they're expected to do

To put your finger on it – to realise just what the problem/point is

To put your foot in it – to say or do something tactless, something which upsets other people

To run before you can walk – to try to do more than you're capable of

To run dry – run out of something (use up all the supplies that you had)

To run on time – to be finished or arrive at an agreed time

To run out of time – not to get something finished in an allotted time

To see it coming – to realise that something is going to happen

To sling your hook – get moving, or die

To soften the blow – try to make bad news seems less unpleasant

To soften up somebody – prepare somebody to receive news you want them to react well to, or to prepare somebody to do a deal favourable to you

To spring a leak (it's sprung a leak) – get a hole in it

To stand on your own two feet – to be able to do things on your own, to be independent

To stick your oar in – to try to help but you might not be welcome

To strike a nerve – to cause pain; to uncover a truth

To strike it lucky – to make a lot of money by good fortune; to be very fortunate

To strike it rich – to make a lot of money

To take a dive – experience bad luck

To think on your feet – think about what's happening and act on it as it happens

To throw the baby out with the bathwater – disregard everything without realising that some things should be kept

To top it off – another event happened, either better or worse than previous events

To trip over your own feet – to be clumsy, trip over for no apparent reason

To turn tail – turn and run in the opposite direction

To turn the place upside down – look everywhere for something (hunt high and low)

To turn up like a bad penny – to keep meeting someone you don't want to meet in places you might not expect them

Took the words right out of my mouth – you said just what I was about to say

Tough as old boots – very tough, able to face physical hardship

Tough nut – someone who shows no feelings, or someone very physically strong

Tough nut to crack – someone (or something) that is so strong, it will be very difficult to change them, or have any impact on them.

Trail blazer – someone who does something that's never been done before

Two's company, three's a crowd – two people can have a good time together but it may feel awkward with three, or the third person may feel left out

Under par – not well; not performing well

Under the thumb – under the control of somebody else, usually said of a partner in a close relationship

Under the weather – feeling sick

Up yours – I don't care about you or what you think

Uphill battle – very difficult task

Upper crust – the upper level of society, the aristocracy

Ups and downs of life – the good and bad times we have in life

Use your head – think carefully about things

Use your manners – be polite, act politely

Want a bigger slice of life – to want more than you've got

Watch out – be careful

Watch your step – be careful where you walk in case there are things you might trip over, or, be careful what you say or do in case it upsets somebody else or gets you into trouble

Watch what you say – be careful about what you say

Way to go – well done

Well there you go – well how surprising

Wet blanket – somebody who is always gloomy and only sees the bad side of any situation

Whacked - exhausted

What's got into you – is there something wrong, you seem upset – implication that you are behaving in an unreasonable way

White as a sheet – to have a very pale face because of feeling sick, faint or frightened

Wild horses wouldn't drag it out of me – nothing would induce me to tell this secret

Wool gathering – day dreaming

Work it out - take time to understand the meaning

Worry wart – someone who worries unnecessarily and excessively about things

Yellow – scared, cowardly

You and whose army – I don't think you can do it all by yourself

You can whistle for it – You don't have much hope, or you are not going to be given it

You light up my world – you make me feel very happy

You scared me half to death – you gave me a terrible fright

You send me – you make me feel wonderful

You set my world on fire – you fill me with loving feelings

You turn me on – I am very sexually attracted to you

You turned the light on for me – you showed me the way

You'd forget your head if it wasn't screwed on – you're very forgetful

You're chicken – you're a coward

You're doing my head in – you're making me feel crazy/overwhelming me

You're not yourself today – you seem different from usual, you're acting differently than you usually do; you don't look well today

You're sprung – I know what you're up to

You've got a long face – you look sad

You've got to earn your moccasins – you have to prove yourself worthy of reward; show you are a man; prove you can do it; act worthy of acknowledgement

Your eyes are bigger than your stomach – to take more food than you can eat – to be greedy

Your wish is my command – I'll do whatever you want

Zip up your lips – don't reveal something someone has told you

Metaphor is used in such a huge way in most conversations that it would not be possible to write down every metaphor used. Those outlined above are a few that I have come across. I was born in 1952 and if you are younger or older than me your experiences of metaphor might be different. They may also be different if you live in another country to that of my experience. I hope that you have found the above useful, whatever your situation.

References

American Psychiatric Association (1994). *Diagnostic and Statistical Manual of Mental Disorders*, Fourth Edition, Washington, DC, American Psychiatric Association.

Lawson (2001) *Understanding ans working with the spectrum of autism: An insider's view*, London: Jessica Kingsley Publishers.

Murray, D.K.C. (1992) 'Attention tunnelling and autism'. In P. Shattock and G. Linfoot (eds) *Living with autism: The individual, the family and the professional*. Sunderland: Autism research Unit, University of Sunderland, UK.

All of the poems contained within this book have been written by Wendy Lawson.

Index

achievements 62–3
activities 135–6
adrenalin 120
agencies 55, 88–9, 92, 124
anger 79–80
assistance, asking for 123–4
attitudes 86
  useful approaches 86–7
Autism and transition 35
Autism: My Gender 81–2
autism spectrum
  cognitive processes 22–4
  diagnosis 9–10
  'triad of impairments' 25

belief systems 100
body language 32, 70–1, 73–4

change 34–8, 118–19
Change 36
childhood 95–6
choice 100–2
closed picture thinking 22–3,
  33–8
clothing 69–70, 117–19
  new items 101, 118–19
community resources 55, 88, 124
connections 91
consequences *see* predicting
  outcomes
constructive comment 63
conversation
  and body language 70–1
  emphasis and context 76–7

explaining needs 30, 53–4,
  102–3
about interests 72–3, 107–8,
  122
signals of interest and
  non-interest 71–2
'small talk' 142
criticism 63

daily living plans 109–11
daily routines 112–14
dairy products 87–8
decision-making 100–2, 132–3
diagnosis 9–10
*Diagnostic and Statistical Manual of
  Mental Disorders* (DSM-IV) 9
diaries 41
diet 87–8
  and mood 120–1
'diffability' 25–7, 57
difference 109, 137–8
'disability' 24–5
dislike of others 78–9
doors 97–100
dreams 60–1

eating *see* food and eating
electronic organisers 31, 41–2
emotional pain 78
emotions
  acceptance of 51
  disguising or concealing 77–80
  factors influencing 120–1
  verbal and non-verbal signals
    70
employment 143–4
  individual skills and 97
energy levels 90–1